Also by Meir Shalev

My Wild Garden

My Wild Garden

NOTES FROM A WRITER'S EDEN

Meir Shalev

Translated from the Hebrew by Joanna Chen

Illustrations by Refaella Shir

Schocken Books, New York

Library of Congress Cataloging-in-Publication Data
Names: Shalev, Meir, author. Chen, Joanna, translator. Shir, Refaella, illustrator.
Title: My wild garden : notes from a writer's eden / Meir Shalev ; translated by Joanna Chen ; illustrated by Refaella Shir.
Other titles: Ginat bar. English
Description: New York : Schocken Books, 2020.
Identifiers: LCCN 2019025765 (print). LCCN 2019025766 (ebook).
ISBN 9780805243512 (hardcover). ISBN 9780805243529 (ebook)
Classification: LCC PJ5054.S384 G5613 2020 (print) | LCC PJ5054.S384 (ebook)
| DDC 892.48/608—dc23
LC record available at lccn.loc.gov/2019025765
LC ebook record available at lccn.loc.gov/2019025766

www.schocken.com

Jacket art by Refaella Sher
Jacket design by Kelly Blair

Printed in China
First American Edition
9 8 7 6 5 4 3 2 1

Contents

In Lieu of a Preface

It was a Sabbath morning in spring. I was packing a picnic basket and studying a map, wondering where to go hiking, when I heard voices coming from my garden.

A man's voice shouted: "Stand still! Right there! Stand still!"

A young woman's voice asked: "Like this?"

A man's voice replied: "Lean against him a little . . ."

A woman's voice instructed: "Look at her. Let them see how much you love her."

Peeking through slits in the shutters, I saw what appeared to be a large white mast, sailing on the red sea of my poppies. I opened the shutters a bit and discovered that the mast was a bridal dress with a bride inside it: a big woman, and lovely in her own way. The groom stood by the bride, a young man, short of stature, thin on flesh, meticulously combed, unshaven with the same meticulousness, dressed in a tight white suit, wearing pointy white shoes and a tie of white and gold. A kind of "bizarre being," as we used to say in my family.

There were two photographers there as well, one on the video and the other on the stills, and a soundman and makeup artist and two older women, one big and the other small, probably the in-laws, and they were all trampling rudely over the poppies and the lupines and the blue thistles that I grow in my garden.

I went outside and shouted, "What are you doing here?"

The group turned sixteen astonished eyes on me.

"Do you mind not interfering?" one of the photographers said, and the other one grumbled, "He can't even see we're filming . . . !"

"You're in my garden, and you're trampling my flowers," I raised my voice.

"Does this look like a garden to you?" the small mother-in-law asked the big one.

"No," said the big mother-in-law to the small one, "it looks to me like the countryside."

The groom plucked up courage. "They photographed my brother here two weeks ago," he announced, "and no one said anything to him."

I ruminated. Which of the two is his mother? The small one, who bequeathed him her height? Or the big one, whom he loved so much that he chose a wife of comparable proportions? So goes the human heart. A heavy shoe tramples your flowers, and you preoccupy yourself with irrelevant thoughts.

"Very true," the big one explained, unintentionally answering my ruminations. "I'm marrying off two sons in one month."

I said, "In three minutes the automatic irrigation system will turn on the sprinklers, and then you'll see whether this is countryside or garden."

I don't have sprinklers in the garden, but fear for their equipment, makeup, hairdos, and fine clothes had an immediate effect: the mothers, the young couple, the film crew—they all beat a hasty retreat, and I returned to the house, puffed up with pride. It's not every day that an amateur gardener receives such a compliment—a bride and groom coming from afar to be photographed among the blooms of his modest garden.

My Wild Garden

A New Place

At the heart of my garden stands the house where I live. I remember very well the day I saw it for the first time. Back then, I was looking for a house outside the city. I wandered through villages and hamlets; I poked around, knocked on doors; I questioned corner-store owners and met secretaries of agricultural cooperatives. I chatted with fathers and mothers and shared secrets with sons and daughters. I had already seen quite a few possible dwellings, but this one I loved at first sight: a small meager house, the kind that looks like what were once called Jewish Agency houses. A modest lawn dying at the front, prickles and dry weeds tumbling around it, and a few ornamental bushes and fruit trees, some of which were about to die of thirst.

The house stood on a slope. I went down and walked around it, and here was the surprise: an expansive, deep landscape that stretched out to the farthest western edges. It began with two plots of cultivated land with a few spears of cypresses at their margins, and above them two ranges of forested hills, dotted with dense impressionistic smudges of variegated green: the pale green of the Tabor oak, the dark green of the Palestine oak, here and there the gleaming green of the carob, and the green of the terebinth—that of the slightly faded Land of Israel terebinth and the more vibrant mastic. And above all this, veiled in the summer haziness of the valley, lay a familiar bluish range that extended from one end of the horizon to the other—the Carmel. Which valley? I don't want to insult anyone, but when I say *the* valley, I am referring to my very own Jezreel Valley.

I turned around and looked back at the house. Because of the sloping nature of the plot, the rear of the house was supported by thin concrete pillars that created a space between the house and the ground below. Someone, I noticed, had built a small wire coop for chickens. I peeked in and saw four small carcasses bedecked in feathers, and they were all as dry as the tin water trough that stood beside them. When he left, that person had abandoned the chickens in their prison, to die of hunger or thirst. But the house filled me with the happiness of a new love, and even this evildoing did not curtail it.

I examined the plants and trees around it: an old pear tree, a dying lemon tree, a shady pecan tree, two oaks and three terebinths, chinaberry, and jacaranda. A hardy prickly pear also grew there, and a crisp marijuana plant, remarkably green against the brown and yellow background. I wondered who might be coming to water it with such devotion? At the front of the house stood a fig tree, its fruit overripe, but when I drew closer to it I saw tiny mounds of fresh sawdust, heralding disaster, piled up by the trunks. A closer look also revealed tunnel openings dug by the fig-tree borer, a harbinger of death that eats through the flesh of the trunk and eventually topples it.

Everything I saw suggested the garden would need much work and forethought. But although I've always loved nature, I had precious little experience in gardening. I was an observer: of my grandfather in Nahalal, and my mother—his daughter—in Jerusalem.

My grandfather was a professional planter who planted a vineyard, a grove, and an orchard on his farm. I loved watching him prune and trellis the grapes in his vineyard. The movements of his hands enchanted me. I was just a child and did not know how to express this in words, but I felt that the movements of a craftsman were the most beautiful movements ever to be embedded within the human body. To this day I enjoy watching carpenters, locksmiths, farriers, stonecutters, bakers—more than watching athletes or ballet dancers.

My grandfather grew up in a Hasidic family in the Ukraine, and when he was old enough to know his own mind, he underwent a religious conversion from the work of God to the work of the land. But my grandfather did not forget his Talmud: the first trees he planted in his yard were olives, pomegranates, and figs, all close to the vineyard. It was no coincidence that these were the fruit trees the Torah included in the seven species that the Land of Israel was blessed with. Alongside the house he planted orange and grapefruit, two more pomegranate trees, and one unbelievable tree that yielded oranges, lemons, tangerines, and other citrus fruits that I do not recall—perhaps grapefruit and, perhaps, according to the storylike nature of my family, avocado or tomato. Either way, that tree aroused awe and excitement within me, and this only increased when I asked my mother how her father had managed to create it. "He's a magician," she said. Years later I discovered it was a perfectly ordinary grafting of bitter orange understock, but my mother's words were already engraved upon me, and the impression has never dissipated.

She herself cultivated a small garden in Jerusalem, where we lived in the Kiryat Moshe housing project. I was about four years old when we first arrived there. Construction of the project had just finished, trees and flowers did not yet grow there, and the place looked like a construction site. But at the front of the apartment block we lived in was a strip of land divided into small plots intended for gardens, and behind it was rocky terrain. My mother followed in the footsteps of her parents. She immediately began to dry the swamps and make the desert bloom: in the front plot she planted dahlias, chrysanthemums, freesias, nice little plants that were nicknamed "summer cypresses," a decorative plant that in those days was widespread and popular and that I no longer see at all, and the wandering Jew that quickly hung down, covering the wooden fence along the sidewalk.

There were no drip irrigation systems back then, and my mother dug holes, hacked out trenches, and watered her garden with a hose and funnel. The practice of watering like that has since disappeared: at the time, passersby would come up and ask to drink from the water in the hose. There were those who drew the nozzle to their lips, and there were those who cupped their hands and drank from the water that pooled there. The former, my mother determined with the derision of a country woman, "drink like city folks" and the latter "know how to drink." In the pocket of every child in the housing complex, attached to the latchkey, was another key with a square depression that opened garden faucets from which to drink and then closed them. This is how we quenched our thirst when walking home from school at noon. There were garden owners who welcomed us and there were those who chased us away with threats and shouts.

In the plot at the back, my mother tended another small garden, fundamentally different from the one at the front. There was nothing but a few square feet of rock, but she was accustomed to hard work. My mother wanted to sow and plant, and she knew how to do it. She brought wheelbarrow after wheelbarrow of earth from the nearby field—today the site of several houses and the Mercaz HaRav Yeshiva—and enriched it with manure that she also collected there, produced by the cows that dwelled in the small cattle sheds of Givat Shaul and grazed by our houses. She planted plum and pomegranate, and in the crevices between the rocks she embedded cyclamen bulbs and seeds. Our neighbor, Amotz Cohen, the teacher and naturalist, planted grapevines in the adjoining plot and fenced them off with prickly pears. Gradually, their gardens took shape.

I went back and contemplated the house I had found and the land surrounding it, and I was sorry that my mother and grandfather and neighbor were no longer with me, to instruct and offer advice. But a few days after I purchased the house, one of the village elders paid me a visit, and I found him to be brimming over with goodness. His name was Yosef Zaira, and like most of the village founders he had also emigrated from Romania. His nickname hinted at this: Puyu—Romanian for "chick."

A few years later, Puyu passed away. I remember him well and feel his absence. He was an educated and entertaining man, a sentimental cynic, a gifted painter, and an expert on fruit trees. In subsequent meetings he taught me a chapter or two on the history of "the great Romania," as he referred to his beloved birthplace, while drinking *ţuică* and playing backgammon, a game at which he excelled.

Now he brought a saw with him, telling me to remove all the dead branches of the lemon tree: "Take them all down! Don't be afraid! It'll all grow again. If only we could get rid of every dead thing inside our own bodies and souls!" I did as he commanded and also dug a ring around the tree for watering.

"Its diameter should be the same as the tree's," Puyu said.

"That wide?" I asked.

"You surprise me. After all, you come from a family of farmers," he said. "Did they never tell you there's always another tree in the earth? The branches are the roots growing downward!"

So I pruned and watered it and the lemon tree recovered. Its shriveled leaves unfurled and opened out, new leaves developed, it flowered and

returned me a favor: an abundance of small lemons, uglier yet more delicious than any lemons I have ever tasted.

I cut and cleared away all the weeds and thistles. I watered and mowed
the lawn, bringing that back to life as well, and I planted a hedge of bougainvillea to separate myself from the road.

But lo, summer ended, autumn passed by, and my first winter in this
new place arrived. Rain fell, and all the seeds sprouted afresh: thistles and
dill, mallow and Spanish golden thistle, dog's tooth and everything else
our forefathers grouped under the hazy heading of thorns and nettles.

I felt like Jason, surrounded by enemies who sprang up from the teeth
of a dragon planted in the earth. I understood that a long and difficult
battle lay ahead of me, and that my enemies were strong and determined
and not about to surrender easily. But the weeks passed, and suddenly
a few cyclamens blossomed by the side of the house, a single daffodil

peeked out, and in the next-door garden something surprising happened that took my breath away: hundreds of red anemones burst into bloom, imbuing the garden with color and turning my northern-facing window into the frame of a magnificent picture.

When the blooming season was over, I asked permission to gather anemone seeds from the neighbor's garden. I also brought cyclamen seeds from the nearby cemetery, hyacinth squill bulbs, corn poppy seeds, Syrian cornflower-thistle and lupine seeds from a friend's garden. I procured bindweed seeds from bushes blooming on the verges of Highway 6. I bought sage seedlings, savory, and wild marjoram in a garden nursery, purple rockrose and white rockrose, as well. The experts call them sage-leaved rockrose and soft-hairy rockrose, but that's what we laymen call them.

That was the beginning. Since then I have added many other wild plants to the garden, some of them sowed from seedlings and others planted. With time I have become quite good at it, but I have never reached the highest standards of gardening. Perhaps I began too late and perhaps I am too busy with other things. Therefore, this book is not a manual or a textbook, either of botany or gardening. It is simply a collection of impressions of a modest wild garden and a gardener who tends it and looks after it, someone who, at a relatively late age, found himself a hobby, and perhaps even a new love.

2

Sea Squill

The two dominant flowers in my wild garden today, each to its own season, are the cyclamen and the sea squill. Both are geophytes, storing food underground, the cyclamen with a bulb, the sea squill with a tuber, and both are perennials and flower year after year. Their flowers are delicate and refined but are also hardy and sturdy and last a long time. And because I am fond of both of them and they need minimal care, and even the mole rat and the wild boar do them no harm, I have planted expanses of them in my garden, and they bring joy to the eye and the heart.

There is one thing I regret: neither one sees the other's blossoming, because they flower in different seasons. The squill blooms in the second half of summer and sprouts green leaves only when blossoming is over. And the cyclamen, aside from a few exceptions I will speak of later, blossoms and sprouts leaves at exactly the same time—winter.

The squill is particularly wondrous to me. A versatile creature, and a tough one that makes do with very little, it lives equally well in valleys and hills, deserts and beaches, in heat and cold, shade or light, and in all types of soil. During the most difficult season, when everything around it yellows and grays, when it is surrounded by dry thistles, and the soil is cracked and arid, the squill produces an erect and mighty scepter topped by a dazzlingly white, radiant inflorescence. It does not simply grow it— when the scepter begins to emerge from the tuber, it advances at an enviable rate of four to five inches a day! Why make such an investment during the hottest, driest, and most difficult season? Because the squill is a smart plant: it blooms at summer's end in order not to compete with other flowers for the attention of insects.

Contrary to what many people think, plants do not produce flowers in order to delight the human heart, nor to be placed in vases or arranged into bouquets and offered to loved ones. Flowers are the genitals of plants, and their blossoms are intended for reproduction. But because they do not possess the ability to move from place to place in order to meet and make contact, the majority of plants rely on insects to transfer pollen from male to female. For this reason, most blossom at winter's end and in springtime when the ground is moist, the weather clement, and there are plenty of insects flying about and swarming around. The insects frequent the flowers, become intoxicated on nectar, and guzzle pollen before transferring it to the next flower they visit.

The catch is that many varieties bloom at the exact same season, thus competing with one another: Who will attract the most insects? Consequently, they make an effort to create tempting and delectable fragrances, alluring shapes and colors, and an abundance of nectar and pollen. One can generalize by saying that in the animal world the male woos the female, and in the plant world both the male and female woo beetles, butterflies, and bees.

The squill employs a different tactic: it stays far from the budding crowd and blossoms at summer's end. On the one hand, this is the most difficult and arid of seasons; on the other hand, it is precisely because of this that the squill is almost the only flower on the ground, or anywhere at all. In my own garden, the modest lily blooms at the same time as the squill. Known also as the small-flowered pancratium, its blossoms are as white as the squill's, and its fragrance is similarly faint, because neither needs to invest in the creation of particularly alluring flowers to compete against others. Insects pounce on them, and more than once I have seen sunbirds perching on the scepters of my squill, wobbling like acrobats on a tightrope or hovering around them, imbibing nectar.

I dare speculate that there is another advantage to this policy: seeds that develop after fertilization do not need to wait months until it rains. They mature only at the end of the summer and are not exposed for any length of time either to the sun's rays, dry conditions, or gluttonous critters.

It is not easy to blossom in such heat and aridity, and this is why the squill is equipped with an expansive tuber and thick, penetrating roots for both absorbing and storing water and nutrients. The large green leaves busy themselves photosynthesizing through spring and winter, thereby doing their share of the upkeep; in summer the leaves completely shrivel up in order not to waste moisture. The squill also knows how to defend itself against hungry animals: it has a bad, burning taste and contains toxins. Only ibex nibble at the edges of its leaves now and again.

Since I have many squill plants in my garden, I am often asked where they came from. The answer—one that surprises those who ask—is that I sowed most of them myself, but some were salvaged when a ditch was being dug for a sewage pipe, and others by the roadside. It so happened that I passed a backhoe loader working there, uprooting and crushing entire clusters of squill, and I gathered them up and managed to take twenty or thirty tubers before the asphalt was poured.

Happy and excited, I remember debating what to do on the way home: Should I plant the whole lot together? After all, I thought, these tubers all belong to the same family and surely want to stay together. On the other hand, perhaps some of them cannot stand each other and want to keep their distance? Ultimately, I asked them. All those who said "together," I planted close together, and all those who screamed "alone" or "not near that one" or who were simply silent—in various other places in the garden. I planted some in the cemetery at Nahalal between my mother's grave and that of her brother, Menachem. I think they are pleased with this arrangement and apparently the squill plants are pleased, too, because they began blooming that very first year and have continued to flourish since then. By the way, I later discovered that the planting of squills in cemeteries is an accepted custom among Arabs, who regard its white color as testimony to the integrity of the deceased.

A large squill tuber usually blossoms the first summer after being planted in a new place. This is all well and good, but the squills I love the most are those I sow myself and for whom I wait patiently to bloom. I follow them from sowing to sprouting, I watch them grow gradually, I wait for them to mature and blossom. Do not make light of this matter: eight or nine years pass from the sowing of the squill to its first flowering! In the first year the seed releases a single leaf, a delicate green dagger, and develops a small and delightful tuber. Year after year it develops and grows, lengthening and broadening its roots, producing scales below and leaves on top, and when it reaches the size of a fist the tuber grows the scepter of a first blossom. After ten years of patient waiting, the first bloom fills the heart with special joy, like the consummation of love after endless anticipation.

By the way, the squill reproduces not only from seeds and backhoe loaders, but also from the development of new tubers under the earth. One day I got resounding proof of this, quite literally. I had placed two large clay pots by the entrance to my house, each one containing two squill tubers. A few years later I happened to be standing right beside them when suddenly I heard a strange noise, a kind of muffled yet powerful popping

sound, and before my very eyes one of the pots ruptured and the soil inside it scattered all over the floor. As I bent closer to retrieve the pair of tubers I had planted there, I discovered a third tuber, still attached to one of the others. It was this extra one that had matured and become swollen, eventually applying enough pressure for the pot to break.

Life with the sea squill has taught me that the amount of blossoming varies. There are lean years and there are fat ones. Folklore tells us that if the squill blooms early and enough tubers put forth scepters and flowers, the coming winter will be a rainy one, and if the flowering is scanty it will be arid. On numerous occasions I have tried my luck predicting the weather according to squill blossom in my garden. More than once I have even risked publishing these predictions in the newspaper—and to this day I have been successful. A few botanists, however, were alarmed and corrected me: it is purely coincidental, they said. The quality of the squill blossom is a result of the previous winter, not the one to come. A tuber that receives adequate water, that grows tall and deepens its roots—that produces plenty of large leaves, to provide it with nutrients and absorb sunlight—stores enough nutrients and goodness and is able to produce an impressive bloom, but it is evidence of past rain rather than a predictor of future rain. I listened, I hung my head, I admitted they were right from a scientific standpoint, but for a number of years my annual weather reports have been more accurate than those of professional meteorologists, and I never argue with success, especially when it is mine.

Aside from insects, the squills attract other tiny critters to my garden—the kindergarten children from my village: year after year, class after class, they arrive with their teacher to see the squills blooming. First I hear them approaching, cacophonous and clamorous, and then I see them: four- and five-year-old girls and boys, all in sandals, shorts, and hats, marching behind their teacher like a flock of indentured geese.

The teacher calls out, "Don't touch, just look!" and the little ones—in contrast to that bride, and her mother, and her future husband and his mother, and the makeup artist, the soundman, and the cameramen, who all trampled across my garden—sit among the squill, and right away the same dialogue from last year begins with the same rhyme.

The teacher: "To whom does this season call?"

The children: "The squill."

The teacher: "And why now?"

The children: "Because it's fall."

And then they sing together "At the New Year, at the New Year," a children's song in which Naomi Shemer describes the sea squill so beautifully, blooming like a candle: "At the New Year, like a memorial candle, the squill lights up the field." And indeed, anyone who sees a blooming squill at dawn or dusk knows that when the sun is at its lowest, the flowers glow like a white-flamed candle. And anyone who makes a habit of visiting the squill empire in nature knows that during these hours he or she will be privy to a particularly spectacular sight.

Similarly, in "The White Squill Candles," the poet Natan Yonatan writes:

> How beautiful then are the squill's candles,
> Lighting up and extinguishing with the sun.

In another poem, "There Are Flowers," Yonatan describes their beauty:

> Did you see such beauty,
> Trembling in autumn's wind?
> A golden field dwindles in the dark,
> Lighting candles of squill.

Due to the radiance of the sea squill's inflorescence, its erectness, height, and hardiness, it was used to demarcate borders in days of yore. The sages even said that Joshua Ben-Nun used it to delineate land belonging to the tribes. And indeed, the squill has obvious advantages as a boundary marker: it is cheap, durable, and renews itself after every disaster. It also has a special advantage for farmers: its scepters grow and bloom precisely in the season when the borders of fields need to be clearly seen—the plowing season. And not only during the right season but during the right hours: in the morning and at dusk, before and after the hottest parts of the day, when the farmer goes out to plow his field, the squill's inflorescence glows, delineating its borders.

On one occasion, I walked out of my house to greet the children and listen to the nature lesson they were enjoying in the garden: Every day, the teacher explained, five new flower rings blossom around the sea squill's scepter. By tomorrow, they'll have wilted, and the five rings above them will blossom, and the flowers that have already blossomed and wilted will soon make seeds.

Why is it important for four- and five-year-old girls and boys to know all this? To tell the truth, it is not that important. Even without this knowledge one can grow up to be a law-abiding citizen with a good profession. Perhaps someone will even come up with a new app to save humanity. But a child who learns things like this at the age of four will be a better person when he or she reaches the age of six, and you cannot underestimate a chance like that.

3

Cyclamen

Cyclamens, as everyone knows, bloom in winter, and so it is with my own. Hikers wandering along the road by my house at this time of year often pause to look at them. Once a woman wanderer stopped and asked me, "How come you've got the plot with the most cyclamens?" The word "got" greatly amused me, and besides that—like the bride and groom who came to be photographed on my property—she could not imagine that even a garden of wildflowers is still a garden and that much work is invested in it: weeding and gathering and sowing and planting.

The cyclamen is loved by all who see it, a commonplace plant that is better known than the squill. It is beautiful and special both as a single flower and in its abundant hues of tight clusters—from the palest of pink, almost white, to deep purple. And I will mention something else here: contrary to what many people think, the cyclamen has a fragrance. A faint and delicate one, admittedly, but fresh and pleasant. When there is just one cyclamen, you must bend over it and draw your nose close in order to enjoy it, but when it blooms en masse, the scent hangs in the air like a translucent, fragrant curtain.

On closer inspection, you discover that the flowers of the cyclamen have an inverted structure. The tip of the pedicel, known as *oketz* in Hebrew—"stinger," the stem that bears the flower—curves like the top of a shepherd's crook and inclines downward, but the petals curve upward, as if repairing the damage. And there is another nice thing about the cyclamen—the fingerprints or, more precisely, the leaf prints. Every cyclamen leaf has a unique and special design on it, and it differs from the design on every leaf of every other cyclamen.

As with the squills, I sowed most of the cyclamens in my garden. I like to sow them in flowerpots and window boxes, and after three or four years I transfer the young bulbs to their permanent residence in the garden. But I also have cyclamens that blossom in sidewalk cracks and holes in rocks, and I sowed them there from the beginning. It is difficult to embed mature bulbs between these cracks but easy enough to insert seeds. Adding a little extra soil is also advantageous—and then the waiting begins. The seed will germinate and the bulb will develop underground, molding its shape to the space available and producing leaves and flowers without complaints or demands. Moreover, the cyclamen does not simply look modest; its requirements are modest, too: all it needs is a bit of sun, well-drained soil, and a grower of plants with infinite patience.

During the first year after sowing, the cyclamen develops a bulb the size of a marble, and a single leaf rises up from it. The leaf is small, no bigger than a thumbnail, but already in the distinctive heart shape of a mature cyclamen leaf. During the second year another leaf appears, and the bulb doubles in size. After three or four years the bulb produces an initial flower and, in years to come, many more will blossom. The bulb continues to grow throughout the cyclamen's life, adding an increasing number of leaves and flowers as the years go by, and this is something unique to the cyclamen—that the older it gets, the more beautiful it becomes.

In my garden there are also colonies of cyclamens I obtained as large, mature bulbs. I call one of these colonies Metula because most of the bulbs concealed there were taken—I stress: at the invitation of the local authorities, and with their knowledge—from an area of land that was turned into a new neighborhood in Metula, the northern town bordering Lebanon. The other colonies, the larger ones, I call Yifat, because I brought the cyclamens that grow there from a slope that is today an extension of Kibbutz Yifat. Back then, the Jezreel Valley's regional council invited its residents to come to the area, which was slated for construction, to pull out bulbs from the earth. What fool would turn down such an offer?

Indeed, I was one of many. There were those who craved a carpet of cyclamens in their gardens, and there were others who merely wanted a *kav,* a small measure of cyclamens, on their balconies or in flowerpots on windowsills. Young parents with small children came to teach their offspring about nature and to instill within them a love for it, and there were also elderly couples, with or without grandchildren. A few Russian immigrants, out picking mushrooms, came to see why we had gathered there, and what a pleasure it was to hear their accents sweetening the Hebrew word for cyclamen, *rakefet,* until it sounded utterly Russian.

There were others who did not know the difference between a cyclamen and a plum, and they dug all over the place and trampled this way and that way over the ground. But lo and behold: in contrast to what happens here on the roads or in the street, it was possible to elucidate and explain things without anyone brandishing a hoe or punching me in the face. There were also those who looked down on us commoners, both human and botanic. One of them explained to me they were looking for "orchids and ophrys." A person like this has a particularly beautiful and noble soul, and regular folks out looking for regular cyclamens and regular anemones will feel justifiably inferior in their midst.

Those who came armed with a spade regretted it. The ground was stony, their blades were wide, and with every thrust they encountered rock. The experienced ones were equipped with a pickax, and they knew to gauge, according to the diameter of the circle of leaves, the size and precise location of each bulb, despite its being hidden underground. They also knew where to land the blade without damaging the bulb. One of them, a skilled and swift worker, toiled near me. After a brief conversation on the advantages of a large pickax (his) and a small pickax (mine), he told me his garden was already full of all sorts of wildflowers, and now he had come to get cyclamens in order to surprise members of the village in which he lived. For a while he had been secretly planting tubers and bulbs and seeds on verges and in public areas, and next year all his flowers would flower and no one would know where they had come from.

"And you're not going to tell them?" I asked.

"No. Only I'll know. It will be a surprise for them." And his face shone with a smile that made him look like one big flower.

I looked at him and recalled Jean Giono's *The Man Who Planted Trees*—a small book published in the fifties of the previous century, translated from French to Hebrew and many other languages—and which still captures readers' hearts to this day. The hero is a shepherd by the name of Elzéard Bouffier who lives in a desolate area between the lower Alps and Provence. The story begins before World War I, when only a handful of hardworking people lived there, charcoal burners and shepherds.

The shepherd Elzéard Bouffier had a big and beautiful dream, and he dedicated his life to its realization: every single day he placed tree seeds in his shepherd's rucksack, particularly acorns of oaks, and as he walked along with his flock he would bury them in the soil. He did this for many years, until a large area became covered by the trees he had sown. The soil was preserved and not swept away, and thus the area came back to life. Flowers bloomed there, birds, animals, and people returned to live there, and miraculously the springs began to flow again, and water gushed along the riverbeds—all this due to the work, dedication, and belief of a single man, a simple shepherd, endowed with a vision and a talent for carrying it out. However, before we forget that this is all the work and imagination of the author, I must add that for years many believed that this beautiful utopia was a true story. There were also those who went to the trouble of traveling there to see the forests and streams, even expecting to meet the shepherd. They were angry at Jean Giono, who eventually admitted that, like all storytellers, he had made it up.

I told all this to the local Elzéard Bouffier and then, taking my bounty, I returned home happily to establish another colony of cyclamens in my garden.

4

Wild Trees

I have already mentioned how I came across a few ornamental bushes and cultivated trees near the house, planted by whoever lived here before me: jacaranda, chinaberry, a large rosebush, a small almond tree, a lilac bush, a pear tree, and a large and overbearing mass of leadwort. I was forced to cut down the chinaberry, of which I will tell more later, and I cut down much of the leadwort and transplanted a fraction of it to a different corner of the garden, to serve as a hedge. The others still grow here, and although they are not wild trees, I let them be.

There are trees of both forest and grove, remains of the natural flora that covered the area before people settled there: two Tabor oaks, two Palestinian buckthorns, one mastic, and three terebinths. I added two Judas trees, two sweet bay seedlings, snowdrop, laurustine, three spiny brooms, two honeysuckles, a few rush brooms, two eastern strawberry trees, and a bear's plum.

Both spiny brooms were destroyed by a murderous tractor driver who was working on the periphery of my garden. That very morning, I showed him the two shrubs and asked him to be careful, and in the evening I found them uprooted and mangled. One Judas tree died soon after it was

planted—I have no idea why—and the second one grew and blossomed, but because it is not the type of Judas tree that produces flowers prior to foliage, the purple blossoms are obscured by its green leaves and it is not the most beautiful of its kind. The plum tree acclimatized well but grows very slowly. One day, when it is larger, it will bloom in white and will be the loveliest tree in my garden.

The rush broom shrubs adapted well, and they flowered with such a bountiful and radiant blossoming that they began to self-sow and spread throughout the garden, and I was forced to uproot their offspring the same way I uproot dog's-tooth grass. The styrax also grew and blossomed and, like the rush broom, it pleases not only the eye but also the nose. The rush broom bears yellow flowers with a sweet fragrance. The styrax bears white flowers with a lovely fragrance, too, but I do not possess the words to describe it. I can only say that the smell is as white as the flower that produces it, and leave the rest to the readers' imagination, or suggest the reader go to the trouble of smelling these white flowers in order to come up with superior adjectives.

Incidentally, the spiny broom contains toxins. Once upon a time, fishermen used to grind them up and scatter them in the Sea of Galilee in order to stun the fish. A shepherd, who came up to my house from the forest asking for cold water, was surprised to see spiny broom growing in my garden. He told me to be careful because "sheep die from that tree and goats just go crazy." I do not know if this story is true, but I left the two spiny brooms where they are, because I do not have a herd yet, neither sheep nor goats, and I myself do not eat their fruit.

A s for the eastern strawberry tree, it usually grows in places that are higher and colder and in soil that is chalkier than I am able to offer in my garden. I know of a number of groves scattered around the Galilee, the Carmel, and the Judean Hills. One of the most beautiful and stunning groves is at the top of Mount Giora, situated above the point where the Refaim and Soreq Rivers meet.

Here and there, exceptionally beautiful eastern strawberry trees grow in solitude. Anyone wanting to reach them must kindly ask where they might be found, and then search far and wide, wearing out one's legs while navigating the way. The effort pays off: the tree's leaves glow, its blossom is lovely, its trunk is smooth and red, and every year the tree sheds its bark, taking on the appearance of a creature shedding its skin. This red color explains its name and is connected to a folktale in which a son murders his father.

My friend Professor Amots Dafni, a man of plants and letters, told me that the largest eastern strawberry trees in Israel can be found in Ein Kinya, east of Ramallah. The biggest one I've ever seen grew in the garden of the botanist Atai Yoffe on Kibbutz Netiv HaLamed-Heh. It is so tall and expansive that its huge branches are considerably thicker on their lower sides to avoid breaking under their own weight. In describing a righteous believer, the psalmist and prophet Jeremiah wrote about a tree like this: "For he shall be as a tree planted by the waters, and that spreadeth out her roots by the river, and shall not see when heat cometh, but her leaf shall be green; and shall not be careful in the year of drought, neither shall cease from yielding fruit"—and who knows, since Jeremiah was a prophet, perhaps he was even referring to that same eastern strawberry tree when he predicted that, in another two thousand five hundred years, the tree would flourish above the hydrophyte pond in the garden of Ati Yafa on a kibbutz named Netiv HaLamed-Heh.

One of the two eastern strawberry trees I planted died a few weeks later. I managed to save its brother, who was also at death's door, and I am proud to say I did it all myself. I first asked the experts, and they told me it's common knowledge that the eastern strawberry tree is difficult to grow and often dies soon after planting, and there is nothing to be done about it. But I didn't give up. I read and researched and discovered that the eastern strawberry tree needs a type of fungus that grows at the root of the tree and which has a symbiotic relationship with the tree known as mycorrhiza. The eastern strawberry tree provides the fungi with nutrients, and the fungi helps the tree to absorb nutrients from the earth. That's nice to know—usually only the parasite benefits from the situation, whereas here each helps the other until they are unable to exist separately.

I surmised that my eastern strawberry trees, purchased in a plant nursery, had not found the fungi they needed in my garden, and because I did not know how to attach fungi to roots, I sat and thought about it, and then thought about it some more, and then, like a happy ending to a children's storybook, I had an idea: I took a shovel, a hoe, and two buckets and drove to an eastern strawberry tree grove I know in the Carmel. I dug for a while and then gathered up a bit of soil from between the trees in the hope that the soil contained that fungi. I returned home, dug gently and carefully around my poor pup of a tree, tipped the soil I had brought back into the hole, watered it, and this time I didn't need the patience my garden has demanded of me on numerous other occasions. Within a few weeks the ailing tree recovered and thrived.

But this was not the end of our trials and tribulations, the tree's and mine. The strawberry tree did indeed begin growing, but rather than growing upward it inclined severely to one side. This kind of growth indicated I had carelessly planted the tree in a place that was too shady, and the tree was striving toward the rays of sun that still managed to penetrate. To correct this, I removed a few oak branches that overshadowed the tree, pruned it a little, and within a short time my eastern strawberry tree grew new upright branches that added to its height, and today—with loving fungi at its roots and a shining sun above its foliage—it continues to develop and redden, and one day it will be a beautiful big tree.

5

Long Gone

When I was a child, I wanted to be a zoologist. Truth be told, I still want to be a zoologist today. Sometimes, although I know it is unlikely, I tell myself and others that one day this is what I might be. Meanwhile, I observe animals in the garden and enjoy it very much. There are all types of winged creatures. And numerous insects, jumpers, hoppers, and flyers: butterflies and beetles and crickets and ants, praying mantises, cicadas, and grasshoppers. And creepy-crawlies: scorpions and centipedes and millipedes and spiders.

I find insects particularly interesting. They differ from us humans in a fascinating and thought-provoking way. Most of their behavioral characteristics are not gleaned through learning or experience but are cemented within them from inception, and the cycle they go through—from larva to mature insect—is something unsurpassed in the development of vertebrates.

I wonder: Does the butterfly remember when it was a larva? Does the larva know that one day it will become a butterfly? And the affable antlion that flies through the air, does it remember how it ate voraciously, ambushing its victims in a trap dug in the sand? And which stage in its life does the mosquito love most? When it is a larva swimming in water or an adult flying through the air? We also pass through stages in our lives, but these stages do not encompass such extreme and definitive contrasts between the corporeal and material stage of eating and growing and fattening up and the brief stage of flight and love. We also raise our offspring and educate them, but we do not lay eggs on leaves and simply take off.

Mankind has cataloged insects through different methods, classifying some as pests and others as beneficial. Both types exist in my garden. The longhorn beetle finished off a large fig tree, and the pomegranate playboy butterfly damages the fruit in the tree after which it is named, year after year. I have noticed that, contrary to these insects, all kinds of bees and beetles pollinate the flowers. There are also more mundane insects that gladden my heart and awaken my curiosity, like the Oedipoda grasshopper. When it alights upon the ground, this grasshopper is difficult to see because of its camouflage. But when it is startled and flutters into the air, the Oedipoda spreads extremely colorful wings—I have seen yellow, blue, and red ones—and then, very conspicuously, flies a few feet up into the air, enticing the eye to follow it. Just before landing, it suddenly closes those wings, extinguishing itself and disappearing instantaneously. The eye, already accustomed to the Oedipoda's vivid coloring, becomes disoriented and loses track immediately.

Once there were plenty of Oedipodas in gardens and fields, but now I hardly ever see them. Butterflies have also become scarce. During my childhood in Jerusalem I saw plenty of them, more than I've ever seen here in the valley. This is strange, since Jerusalem's entire essence stands in contrast to that of a butterfly, to its lightness and colorfulness. It seems that today most of the fliers in Jerusalem are ravens, stones, curses, prophecies, and swallows, but fifty and sixty years ago the city was packed full of white cabbage and swallowtail butterflies—a large and magnificent butterfly whose larvae I raised at home, encouraged by my mother and agreed upon by my father. I fed them on fennel stalks I found in a nearby field. I tracked their eating and development, their metamorphosis and emergence from chrysalis to butterfly. At first, they flew around the house, and eventually they flew right out of the window. Once outside, they changed their flight instantly, the moment the sun's rays cast warmth and life through them.

To my great sorrow, the firefly is an insect that has almost disappeared. In my childhood there were plenty of fireflies that glowed at night in gardens. I would collect a few of them in the palm of my hand and their light would shine through my fingers. Once—only once, soon after I arrived here—I spied one in the garden. My heart swelled with joy. I hoped this was a sign that more and more fireflies would appear. But my expectations were dashed. There are no fireflies to be seen today, and I deeply miss them.

There are also reptiles in the garden: snakes and agamas and other lizards. Here and there a tortoise appears, but these occasions are few and far between. There are also skinks, legless lizards that are perhaps a transitionary stage between lizard and snake. For some years, the biggest of all skinks lived in my garden, an enormous creature known as a scheltopusik. It can grow to three feet in length; its skin is smooth and shiny and its body firm. At first glance it looks like a snake, but it is nothing more than a huge skink. The scheltopusik is not venomous, of course, but is very strong. When you hold it you can feel its strength as it strives to extract itself from the grip of your hand. All this is a little less entertaining for the scheltopusik, of course, because at a certain moment it stops struggling and sprays particularly repulsive urine and feces in all directions. For this reason, I do not recommend playing this game for too long. One day, the scheltopusik vanished, and that was that. I was sorry but not surprised. There was a time when species disappeared gradually over eons, but today—if a person is attentive and watchful—this can be witnessed in a single generation.

Aside from the butterflies and fireflies I have already mentioned, there were once winter puddles filled with toads in Jerusalem, and huge flocks of starlings that performed spectacular aviation shows. The vultures that nested in the Carmel would glide over the valley, hyenas' laughs rose up from fields at night, scrub robins spread red tails in thickets, and on winter mornings I enjoyed a very special alarm call: the tap-tapping sound of the song thrush, formerly known in Israel by its Latin name, *turdus,* as it smashed snail shells on the sidewalk.

There were also joyful flocks of goldfinch back then, frequent victims of greedy hunters, who crossbred them with canaries and put their off-spring in cages. I also fondly remember the tortoises, roaming in their dozens through the field near our Jerusalem neighborhood, where it was possible to hear the clicking of their shells during the mating season. Today, even in the nature reserve near my home in the valley, I rarely see them. The tree frogs, those small green affable creatures that appear in the garden, and green lizards too—beautiful and elegant animals—have diminished in number, as have whip snakes.

Many of these small and beautiful reptiles are exterminated by both stray and domesticated cats, who kill them with a mighty paw and out-stretched claw, not merely out of hunger but out of a lust for hunting and an urge for amusement that is almost human in its cruelty, and—either out of ignorance or convention or a self-righteous sense of political cor-rectness, or perhaps because cats arouse a lot more tender feelings than frogs and lizards—we ignore the continuous and systematic massacre of other creatures.

It is not only animals that are disappearing. The oak forest facing my home is a remnant of a huge forest that once covered the Lower Galilee, the Menashe Hills, and much of the Sharon area. The Ottoman Empire fed its steam engines on this forest, destroying much of it. Deforestation for agriculture and the coal industry also did its part here, and today there are only three remaining areas: Beit Keshet, Alonei Aba, and Alonei Yitzhak. But small groups of oak, and also solitary oaks, are scattered here and there throughout the previously forested area. In the Jezreel Valley you can still see large solitary oaks in the heart of agricultural fields, left there to provide shade and respite for husbandmen. Who knows? Perhaps one day this land will once again be covered with the ancient forest, and bears will roam through it, and a lion will rise up from the swelling of the Jordan, and who will not fear its roar?

6

Work Tools

There are not only flowers and bushes and trees and animals in the garden, but also a gardener who works there and who requires work tools for that garden. Some of them are as simple and as ancient as a pickax and a hoe; others are modern and sophisticated like the computerized irrigation system that I have never managed to fathom or activate without assistance. Twice a year, at the beginning of winter and beginning of summer, I hire a professional gardener who stops and starts it for me, because no matter how much I try to do it myself, I always manage to delete the irrigation program and have no idea how to reset it.

And there are work tools that are somewhere between a hoe and a computer, like the power scythe. I know how to operate this tool but expend much time and energy installing the cutting wire correctly, and even more time looking for the cocked spring, which always flies out of the rotating head during installation. This spring has its own ritual: it shoots out from between my hands as I work, falling and vanishing into the flora. It vanishes completely, purposefully concealed by the weeds. They have good reason: this power scythe is intended to obliterate them from the face of the earth.

To my great regret, I am no handyman. Whenever I try to repair one thing, I damage something else. My uncles and cousins, just as in the song "I have an uncle in Nahalal, and he can do it all"—and also moshavniks and kibbutzniks and those who served in the army with me—all know how to service a tractor and a jeep, install and repair water and electric systems, weld, do carpentry, erect a brick wall, cast a concrete floor, and they achieve all this quickly, confidently, without blundering or getting dirty.

Each one of them carries his own personal set of work tools in his pockets, the indispensable kinds that are carried everywhere. Today, it is invariably a Leatherman, but in my youth and childhood it was a pair of pliers, and sometimes a monkey wrench, known in Hebrew as a Swedish key and affectionately nicknamed "the little Swede."

I recall a joke that people would tell back then, about three moshavniks who argued over which is the best work tool and should always be kept at hand.

The first said: "I take a Swedish key with me everywhere—it opens everything."

The second said: "I prefer an English key—it opens everything."

The third one said: "I prefer a Russian key."

"What's a Russian key?" his two friends wondered.

"A ten-pound hammer," he explained, "which opens everything."

Alas, the Swedish key and pliers and even the ten-pound hammer continuously drop from my hands, and almost always hit my toes. As for the Leatherman, I prefer my Swiss Army knife because it has a corkscrew—that is to say, its inventor recognized that man was born not only to toil. But I also have a work tool at hand which I carry in the pocket of my gardening overalls whenever I go down to the garden. This tool has no name, and so I'll describe it briefly: It is a piece of plastic that resembles the handle of a screwdriver, and there is a small, hollow protrusion at one end which has a dual function: to pierce holes in water hoses in order to make water drippers and to wedge small spigots into holes pierced by woodpeckers.

The woodpeckers do not peck the hoses out of spite or thirst—that is done by wild boars and jackals that gnaw at the same hoses in order to drink—but because of an error they are making. The zoologist Professor Yossi Leshem, Israel's first and foremost ornithologist, explained to me that the sound of water rushing through hoses is perceived by the woodpecker to be the very sound made by a worm in a tree. Furthermore, the woodpecker regards the outer layer of the hose to be as flimsy as a blade of grass. If I could only persuade the woodpeckers to peck the hoses solely in places where holes are needed, both functions of my tool would be unnecessary. But I have been unable to do this, and so I carry it in my pocket every time I go into the garden. To my joy, I am able to use it with relative ease, and to my sorrow I am frequently forced to use it.

In truth, the amateur gardener should carry a few more tools and gadgets in his pockets: pruning shears, a penknife, a small hoe, a spade, drippers, all kinds of connectors and dividers, a jar of black ointment, and a sturdy trash bag. But the Americans have not yet invented overalls that possess pockets suitable for all this, and the Swiss have yet to invent a pocketknife that performs all these tasks. So I bought myself a box for my work tools, and I placed inside it everything enumerated above. I am very fond of this toolbox, and it seems the toolbox is fond of me too, because once or twice a week it joins me on a tour of the garden: I prune, uproot, plant, smear here and clear there, install and repair, and it waits patiently for its next task. The box also serves as a seat for me when I have something or other to do while sitting, and it only has one problem, that my most beloved tool cannot be placed inside it. On the other hand—the box can be placed inside *it,* because the tool I love most is the wheelbarrow.

I will not underrate the importance of the wheelbarrow in my life and the affection I feel toward it. Thanks to the wheelbarrow, I really appreciate the Chinese, who invented it, according to popular opinion. More precisely, not all the Chinese invented it but one specific Chinese man—a general who required it for military purposes two thousand years ago. His wheelbarrow was much larger than ours, and the wheel was located in the middle rather than the front of the barrow. A wheelbarrow with a central wheel can carry a load far heavier than that wheelbarrow we are familiar with today, because the wheel carries the entire weight, and the operator takes no part in the carrying, but it is more difficult to maneuver.

Plenty of water has flowed under the Yangtze River since then, and today the working man has at his disposal two-wheel wheelbarrows and even motorized wheelbarrows, but the simple wheelbarrow, familiar to all, still exists and it functions the good old-fashioned way. It was, and still remains, a kind of bathtub with two handles and a pair of legs on one side, and a single wheel on the other. The user stands between the handles like a horse standing between the shafts of a cart, but, unlike a horse, the user pushes rather than pulls.

Maneuvering the wheelbarrow is as simple and intuitive as riding a bicycle and, just like riding a bicycle, can be improved and made more professional—to tilt when turning, for example, and to thus improve the angle of steering and the diameter at which it is rotated. Indeed, the wheel is not visible to the eye, but acquired experience gives the operator a sense of where the wheel is.

Since purchasing the wheelbarrow, I have transported soil, stones, firewood, sacks of compost, sand and cement, flowerpots, trash and junk, weeds I uprooted, foliage I trimmed, crates of books from the car to my study, and my firstborn granddaughter, who at the age of three asked for her first wheelbarrow ride. I am not utterly certain as to whether the aforementioned Chinese general intended all this, but the wheelbarrow did not object and the little girl was as happy as a lark.

Every time I use my wheelbarrow, I wonder how I ever lived without it and am impressed by the ingenuity concealed within its incredibly simple structure. The years have made no significant changes to it. On the contrary, they have only refined and improved it, and as an ancient work vehicle, it has character, balance, and a maturity that not only benefits me but also gives me pleasure. And why mince my words? I believe that everyone, not only gardeners and farmers and builders, should have a wheelbarrow in their house. With small alterations in structure, pots and dishes can be brought from table to kitchen sink, a stack of books by the bed can be returned to shelves, washing transferred from washing machine to clothesline, a partner, male or female, who fell asleep by the television can be brought to the bedroom, where the handles will be lifted up and he or she will be poured into bed.

The wheelbarrow is a direct and natural continuation of the body. In this it resembles the hoe, the scythe, and the sickle—they, too, are ancient agricultural tools that have undergone no radical change for thousands of years and that I also use in the garden. With the sickle I crop weeds in places where it is impossible to get close enough with the power scythe. Hold it in your right hand if you are right-handed or with the left if you are left-handed; with the other hand grasp a bunch of weeds tightly, and then simultaneously pull it out while cutting.

As a child, I watched my uncles harvesting corn and durra with sickles. They harvested the alfalfa and clover with an ordinary scythe, not a mechanical one. That scythe appeared magical to me. Its blade, close to the ground and hidden among the stalks, could not be discerned with the eye. Only the bowing of the plants could be seen and the whisper of the cutting heard, and every few minutes the harvester pulled a small file out of his pocket to sharpen the blade with precise, measured movements.

As mentioned earlier, the contemporary scythe, sickle, and hoe still resemble their forefathers of ancient Egypt and Mesopotamia, and so, too, the pickax and shovel, but the metal they are fashioned from today is far superior and much sharper. This is even more pronounced with regard to what we call here the Japanese saw, a magical instrument with which I cut branches much thicker than the span of the jaws of the largest pruning shears. The quality of the steel teeth and the angles of their sharp blade surprise me anew every time I use them. A branch as thick as my arm yields to it within five or six motions, and even an amateur like myself, with limited technical abilities, can appreciate a tool of such high quality.

And there's another gardening tool, a very practical one that cannot be found in stores or garden nurseries. I do not know its name, but after having it explained to me I was able to set it up myself: take a metal pipe that is seven feet long and two inches in diameter, and insert the blade of a pickax into one end. With a few vertical blows, the blade can be embedded within the hose, and its other end, the one that protrudes, deepens and widens planting holes that the pickax and hoe are unable to advance through without hitting the walls of the hole. If anyone among the readers is familiar with the tamping iron, known in these parts as the *balamina,* the ancient stonecutter's rod—I can tell you that this gardening tool is the *balamina* of soil.

Apart from all these implements, most of which were originally used in agriculture, I regularly use work tools from the kitchen: a wooden rolling pin helps me to thresh a variety of seeds; and I also make use of a number of sieves in order to separate seeds from chaff.

Once, Hebrew speakers used the word *nafa,* a sieve with fine holes used for sifting flour, and *kevara,* a sieve with wider holes, and *mesanenet,* a strainer that is smaller in diameter than the others. We no longer mill grain at home and hardly ever use a sifter in the kitchen, and we further describe all of these with the one word left over from this holy trinity— *mesanenet.* But a garden like mine, more primitive than other gardens, with plants far simpler and more ancient than cultured plants, demands old-fashioned tools and primeval names and simple craft. And so I use a *nafa* for sifting poppy seeds, a *kevara* for Agrostemma seeds, and a *mesanenet* for the chicken soup I prepare, because I like mine perfectly clear.

7

Mole Rat

Facing my house is a tilled field, and every year it shifts from stubble yellow to plowed brown and from that to the green of germination and growth. Sometimes this is the radiant green of corn and sometimes the bluish green of the vetch, and now—the month of January—as I stand on the balcony and gaze out at the view, it is the soft inviting green of sprouting wheat, punctuated by dark brown mounds of earth that have arisen almost overnight. These are molehills, but they are not the usual mounds that mole rats leave behind. There is something about them, something that indicates a great subterranean drama.

The mole rat is a reclusive creature that disapproves of all other beings and particularly abhors its own kind. Most days it digs itself an underground system of tunnels and chambers that serve as lodgings and provide for everyday needs and—if it is a female mole rat—a place in which to raise the next generation. The mole rat defends its kingdom with ferocity, widening and deepening it through hard labor. It gets rid of the soil with upward motions and, consequently, mounds are formed above its living quarters. Usually they are scattered haphazardly over the area, but the ones I see now draw a straight and purposeful line for several dozens of feet along the wheat field. In other words, this particular mole rat is striving toward a goal, or, more precisely, this is a male mole rat digging in order to get to a female one.

Since I am also an animal of the male persuasion, I will describe the situation as follows: there are two men here, one who stands upright, on the balcony, looking at the view, and another who crawls under the earth and cannot see anything at all. They both belong to the mammal department, they both have four limbs, they both have a heart and brain, lungs and a stomach and a backbone, but I stand loitering, enjoying the brilliance of a pale winter sun, the blossoming of cyclamens and the fragrance of daffodils in the garden, while he labors inside a dark and suffocating tunnel. On journeys and hikes usually taken in daylight, I see the terrain through which I move, sometimes I even use a compass and map, while the mole rat knows to calculate and maintain the azimuth of his heart's desire even in complete darkness.

All this is very nice. They say that love is blind, and some people even say love causes blindness, but the mole rat is born blind and lives in a dark environment. Evolution has sharpened his sense of smell and hearing but rendered him sightless. In spite of this, he will reach his heart's desire with wondrous precision. She won't see him, he won't see her, but in this pitch darkness, and after so much solitude and effort, he will be sure he has arrived at his Rachel even if she is a Leah mole rat, and the next day no morning will shed light upon them or say he erred.

How does he know where she is? What makes him think she will agree? And how does he find his way with such precision? In fact, mole rats communicate with one another by knocking their heads against the tunnel ceiling, and the knocking sound traverses hundreds of feet of deep earth. He deciphers her knocking—"I'm ready"—and he soon thumps back, "I'm coming!" and on the way he hears the thumping of another male or two sending the selfsame announcement and knows that, before the arousing event my grandmother named *consumatzia,* he can expect a battle.

I know all this as well, because, although I lack the sharp ears of a mole rat, I also lack its dulled eyes, and I am capable of distinguishing two more lines of mounds also headed for the same spot. But with all the sympathy and appreciation I have for the efforts that male mole rats, and men in general, are willing to invest on their way to love, in the depths of my heart I hope that those wooing mole rats will fail, and if they somehow succeed in reaching Madam Mole Rat, I hope they fall in the battle for her affections before one of them impregnates her. All this is because one of their offspring may reach my garden and do its worst, as has already happened.

Thus far are the romantic zoological ruminations, among others, on the small, determined, solitary, and blind males who choose to abstain from light, scenery, blossoming, and—aside from the annual subterranean love escapades that I have described here—they also abstain from any social life, not to mention love life. Now I will tell you about the damage they do to my garden.

Despite its violent and malicious misanthropic temperament, the mole rat is vegetarian, and because it destroys roots and bulbs, and at the same opportunity also moles molehills—farmers and gardeners regard it as an absolute terrorist. As for me, the molehills do not bother me in the least. I know that owners of ornamental, landscaped gardens, particularly those with lawns, are horrified by these mounds of earth. But my garden is a wild one, rough and ready, messy and grass-free, and I even find a sense of grace in these molehills, part of the garden's natural landscape.

The roots and bulbs it destroys are another thing altogether. A few years ago one of them made itself at home in my garden, and I well recall the day I saw it wreaking havoc there. At the time I was standing on the same balcony, looking at the blue blossoming of the lupines, when suddenly I noticed they were all erect and silent except for one, which was moving from side to side as if swaying in a soft wind. My curiosity was aroused. I continued watching it and, after a few seconds, the lupine lurched to one side and fell to the ground. I went down there and lifted it up, and the lupine snapped out of the soil as if utterly rootless. I inspected it and saw that, indeed, it had none, because the root had been eaten up to the neck.

I regretted its death, of course, but took comfort in the knowledge that lupines are annuals and they all die anyway at season's end. But then the mole rat discovered the truly desirable delicacies: my buttercups and gladioli. Both are perennial flower bulbs, and as already mentioned with regard to the cyclamen and squill, I waited patiently for some years after sowing them until they grew bulbs large enough to produce flowers. At that point it became clear to me that it was not only I who had waited, but the mole rat, too, and when the bulbs reached the size and taste that he fancied, the mole rat finished them off.

I am usually a man of peace and I hate war, but I am not a pacifist and do not believe in the theory of turning the other cheek. There are occasions and situations in which a man has to fight back or even instigate a fight, for example when his defenseless loved ones are devoured in front of his eyes. And in the special case of mole rat as aggressor, what we are facing here is a veritable war between the sons of light and darkness. And in general, all kinds of enemies lurk in the garden, dangerous to the flora and even dangerous to its owner, but only one of them is worthy of the title "saboteur"—none other than the mole rat.

There are a number of popular methods of fighting the mole rat. The first stage for all these methods is exposing the opening to one of its tunnels. This is not difficult: dig out one of the molehills and under it you will find such an opening, maybe even three or four of them. Now there are a number of options open to you. The most conventional and stupid of them all is to insert a water hose into the tunnel and turn on the faucet full blast.

Anyone who has taken this measure knows that the outcome is always the same: all rivers run into the tunnel, yet the tunnel is not full. The mole rat does not flee but waits comfortably in one of the upper chambers it habitually prepares in case of winter flooding. The water permeates the soil, the mole rat returns to its work, and the gardener receives from the water company—in itself an enemy—a bill befitting a swimming pool.

A different method recommended to me involves inserting the droppings of predators into the tunnel. The smell is supposed to frighten the mole rat enough to drive it away from its home. Unfortunately, there are no leopards or lions where we live and, when I tried this method, I had to make do with dog poop. Indeed, the mole rat did not like the procedure, but, on the other hand, it did not leave home. It worked and cleaned through the night, and the next morning I found the droppings outside the tunnel, and beside them a fresh mound.

The third method may well horrify those with a historical awareness, as well as the noble minded: the hose of an inflatable jack is attached to a car's exhaust, the other end is shoved into the mole rat's tunnel, and the car's engine is started.

"Sounds terrible," I said to a friend who recommended this method to me.

"Don't worry," he said, "they don't die from it. The minute they smell the exhaust fumes, they escape. Twenty minutes more at two thousand four hundred rpm is enough for the stink to linger throughout the tunnel, and that's it—the mole-rat problem is solved once and for all."

He promised me this, noting that he had already done so in his garden and that it worked. The truth? It sounded convincing and even tempting, but in spite of the temptation I decided there are things that Jews should not do. Instead of this I used a method that arouses fewer associations, namely the laying down of burning coals at the entrance to the tunnel. Animals are terribly afraid of fire, and the mole rat will swiftly run away, or so I was assured. However, my mole rat did not run away but instead built a barrier of soil close to the tunnel's entrance, in front of the coals I placed there.

After all these methods had been considered and discarded, or tried and found lacking, and after further bulbs and tubers and roots had been demolished, I realized this was a real war, a war in which only one side could survive. I had a few tactics to choose from. One was the placing of poisoned tablets specifically for this purpose in the mole rat's burrow. When moistened they release a poison that is supposed to kill the mole, or the gardener, depending on who is closer and which way the wind is blowing at the time. I tried, we both survived and remained alive, and I decided to resort to something I remembered from my adolescent days: a face-to-face battle, an ambush at the entrance to the tunnel.

This method is based on the fact that the mole rat, as soon as its home is broken into, attempts to seal itself off, and from there, above the break-in, the gardener waits with raised hoe. All this is easy to say but very difficult to implement. After an hour and a half in this distressing position the gardener realizes that the damage made by the mole rat to his backbone is far more serious and painful than the damage wreaked on the gladioli and buttercups. After a further hour he understands that the damage he is causing himself is greater than the damage the mole rat is causing him, and after a further hour, when the mole rat—suspicious and longanimous—finally turns up, it does not come out and offer its head on the chopping block but instead pushes earth out of the tunnel with its snout. This is the moment to gauge its location and bring the hoe down with all one's might in the hope that it will penetrate the layer of earth and strike the mole rat. However, the gardener usually misses or hits a rock that is also under the earth, and the blow is so terrifying that all his bones praise the Lord. The mole rat, who has already experienced such events in its life, chuckles to itself and continues crawling through the depths of its home, and the gardener also crawls home or, more to the point, to his bed, where he lies and then makes himself an urgent appointment with the physiotherapist.

Another ancient and violent method is the use of a firearm known as the mole cannon. The mole rat is not a mole—there are no moles in Israel—but neither is the instrument a cannon, but more a kind of improvised pistol: a short piece of metal pipe is used as the barrel, and a firing pin equipped with a spring and safety catch pulled forward beyond its tip, and every touch to it activates the mechanism and discharges a shot.

This hellish device cannot be found in stores. To get one you go to an elderly moshavnik who throws nothing away, you look in his storeroom for one of these cannons from the British mandate, and meanwhile you hear stories, anecdotes, and political analyses on the State of Israel from him, with illustrative comparisons to the forties of the previous century. But as you will already have noted, the destruction of a mole rat is not just any old operation, and it contains several levels of danger and sacrifice.

Ultimately you find a cannon, put a pellet from a shotgun in the muzzle procured from another acquaintance, who also has something to say about back then and right now, ask the inquisitive and the admirers and the advice givers to watch from afar, just in case, expose the tunnel opening, and put the apparatus in place. It is best to do so when the barrel is facing in, of course, and to cock the firing pin only when the cannon is in place. The mole rat is supposed to come up in order to close the tunnel and in doing so will touch the tip with its snout or paw, trigger the mechanism, and in fact commit suicide by gunshot. We're talking about real firearms, and thus in many instances this adventure ends in serious injury. Not the mole rat's. Yours.

Despite the fact that by now I would be happy to destroy the mole rat with a real cannon, I have never come across a mole cannon, and evidently this has saved me from enormous misfortune. But then I met a zoologist specializing in mole rats. I recounted my tale of woe and he told me that in the depths of winter, close to giving birth, the female mole rat prepares a nursery for her babies, a kind of subterranean residence with a larder and bedroom.

"If the mole rat in your garden is female, you'll easily find the nursery," the zoologist promised me, "because the molehill above it is three times larger than other molehills. And when you open it, you'll find all your gladioli and buttercup bulbs, classified and neatly arranged, and after you've touched her holy of holies, the female mole rat will run away and never come back."

I looked for a mound triple the size—and there was none. I opened mounds double the size—and found nothing in them. Frenzied, I dug out a regular-sized mound, and after changing clothes—whenever I dig the earth I always strike the water pipe—I sat down on a nearby rock, looked around me, and thought about everything that had happened. I pondered myself, my behavior, and the destruction I had sown in the garden: Here I am, a grown man, usually responsible, who functions in a reasonable manner from a professional point of view, and in most cases from a social point of view as well, and suddenly he—I mean I—concedes precious working hours, the reading of a good book, recreation with his offspring, and dedicates entire days to the brisk digging of his garden, mining ugly potholes and inflicting damage upon himself, the irrigation equipment, and his surroundings, and all this for an ugly sightless creature the size of a sweet potato. So who's the maleficent animal here? Is it the mole rat or me?

I stood up, renounced my righteousness, relinquished my self-respect, and overcame my vengeance. I pulled the survivors out of the earth—the gladioli and buttercups that were left—and transferred them to planters and pots. Since then the mole rat and I are no longer at war but rather manage a conflict, and I sow, sprout, and grow my buttercups and gladioli

only in this way, safe from the enemy's teeth and hunger. This is also the reason I do not plant asphodel in my garden, because they say it is very popular with mole rats. It's true, I did not vanquish, nor did I win, and the saboteur continues his work underground. But I enjoy the flowers that grow above, so how bad can it be?

8

The Mukhraka

There are two types of horizons. The elusive, illusive one that appears at the plain's edge, and my own horizon, which has a sharp border of vision, genuine and clear, disappearing or blurring only on days of fog or haze.

This horizon is the Carmel, rising up almost eight miles west of my home. There are a number of communities and roads that lie between us, but the forested hills close to me conceal all this from my eyes and offer me a pleasantly deceptive picture of a land empty of people and an illusion of space and solitude. The only signs of a community to be seen are the northeastern edge of Tivon and the eastward-facing houses of Isfiya above the Carmel.

The Carmel is lit up in the morning by the rays of the rising sun, when I can distinguish the ravines and gullies sketched within it. In the afternoon the sunlight is directed toward me, and the mountain becomes a solid bluish-gray mass. In the evening the sun sets beyond it, and it darkens, blackens, and disappears.

The most prominent point above the Carmel Range is the Mukhraka. This is not its highest peak, but it appears to be so from my house. The place is named after the Carmelite monastery Dir el-Mukhraka, which is very close by, but it also has the official and correct Hebrew name of Keren Carmel. The State of Israel gave it this name, but the citizens of the State of Israel do not use it. Why not? Because the survival of words is similar to the struggle for survival of animals and plants: only the fittest and most successful make it, while the others perish. In spite of the respect citizens of Israel feel for their language and state, apparently they have a problem saying: "Let's go to Keren Carmel." Perhaps this is because Keren Carmel sounds more like the name of a young and energetic lawyer than the name of a place, but perhaps it is simply because it sounds natural and nice, munificent and melodious, to say: "Let's go to the Mukhraka," and the heart and mouth do not feel the need to change the name to anything else.

But there is another reason, and perhaps not everyone is aware of it: it is precisely the Arabic name Mukhraka that preserves the Jewish tradition connected to this peak, rather than the Hebrew Zionist name Keren Carmel. The meaning of the word *mukhraka* is "place of fire." The name was given to this place after the biblical story of the prophet Elijah, who, according to tradition, competed against the prophets of Baal and managed to do what they themselves could not: to bring down fire from the heavens in order to burn wood and sacrifices on the altar that was specially built for this competition. This fire proved that our own Lord, and not Baal, is the only true God. But the Jewish state, which strives to banish Arabic names both from the map and from consciousness, gave the place the Hebrew name of Keren Carmel and in doing so erased the Jewish heritage that was so precisely preserved by the Arabic name. Undoubtedly, we live in a very complicated and irrational region.

Bringing down the fire and burning the wood and sacrifices were just the first stage in the competition between Elijah and the prophets of Baal. The second stage was far more important: a competition to bring down rain—the first rain after a terrible three-year continuous drought. And

sure enough, after the fire "a little cloud, like a man's hand," rose up, and after that a heavy rain fell, the work of the God of Israel and its prophet, and not of Baal, the official rain bringer of the Canaanites.

The competition between Elijah and the prophets of Baal, who went there that day in their multitudes, had enormous significance. Just as one goes to a doctor who specializes in knees or an engineer who specializes in installation or a lawyer who specializes in criminal law—the people of Israel came to Baal when there was a drought, because Baal was a specialist in everything to do with rain. There is a certain logic to this: in pagan pantheons there were gods specializing in rain and others in sun and wind and sleep and war and medicine, rather than a kind of One Jewish Lord God who claimed to know everything.

As an aside, I must mention the first test of God as supplier of water. During the period of wandering through the desert, God produced water from a rock rather than from the heavens. In my humble opinion, this event indicated to all His believers that, with all due respect to God in particular and monotheism in general, God was not such a specialist in rain. It will thus be of no surprise to learn that they now turned to Baal, who in this case can be called a *baal miktzoa,* a "professional," who did not pretend to solve all the problems of humanity throughout the world but was dedicated to certain well-defined problems of his believers in this land.

Despite everything I have said here, Elijah and God gained a great victory on the Mukhraka. Fire followed by rain came down from the heavens, and Elijah was quick to use the opportunity to slaughter four hundred and fifty Baal prophets in the Kishon River. We could have been proud of this story, relating it to our children generation after generation, but the real ending to the story is different: Three thousand years later I look at the Mukhraka from my garden and chuckle to myself, because in spite of God's victory, the plants I grow in my garden come under the Hebrew heading of "Baal farming" rather than "God's farming," since this is how the Hebrew language refers to crops that are not artificially irrigated but watered exclusively with rainfall. In other words, the Hebrew language determined that at the end of the day it was Baal who triumphed: it acknowledges Baal as the bringer of rain and not the God of Israel.

Funnily enough, Hebrew preserved the belief in Baal, Arabic preserved the victory of the God of Israel, and the State of Israel determined a name for the Mukhraka that makes you forget the entire story—Keren Carmel.

9

Ants

Most of the animals I encounter in my garden are visitors who come and go. But there are also permanent residents: a bevy of jaybirds, a pair of tufted titmice, and numerous subterranean creatures—wolf spiders, who burst forth from their web-padded dens to pounce upon their victims, and the mole rat (my longtime enemy, cursed be his name) and the earthworms (good old friends) and the ants, who build nests in my garden and pave their own way. They are neither enemies nor friends, but we enjoy a stalwart relationship together—because the mole rat and the earthworms are concealed from the eye and the spiders come and go, but the ants and I have been good neighbors for years.

I am unable to name all the ants that live in my garden. But I distinguish between the delicate reddish ants who pile moist earth around the entrance to their nest, and the small black ones whose pungent, acidic smell fills the air. There are also pale brown ants, large and very nimble, that sometimes enter my house and do as they like, and there are black ants, also large and nimble, whose abdomens are positioned on their backs, and I am certain they prey on other ants.

I live peacefully with all these ants, and if it turns out that a few of them have infiltrated my house and entered into the sugar business with me, I do not call a home pest exterminator. Only once was I forced to react, when ants built a nest in a flowerpot that stood on the front porch, and a purposeful and energetic convoy was put into motion, running to and fro with supplies between the flowerpot and the kitchen.

This was an extraordinary nest. The entrance to it was through the drain at the bottom of the flowerpot, and the ants climbed up it and did not climb back down as one might imagine. I decided to expel them before they discovered just how good it was and began settling in other flowerpots and setting a bad example to others. I took the flowerpot and placed it, along with its inhabitants, at the edge of the forest. A few weeks later, I went back to examine the flowerpot and discovered the ants had indeed moved out.

The most noticeable ant in the garden is the messor ant, and I sometimes watch it and try to track its behavior. It has four nests in my garden, all of which were here when I came and which I guess will still be here after I leave. Nothing grows in the vicinity of these nests, but I make no move to chase away the inhabitants and, I must stress, they treat me with patience. They do not wage war against me, nor do I pick fights with them. I acknowledge that the garden is theirs, too, and that I am outnumbered, not to mention the combative capabilities and characteristic sense of self-sacrifice inherent in these ants, neither of which I possess.

We often work together in the garden. We have not yet reached a level of cooperation, but we work alongside each other and perform similar tasks: they bring seeds to their granary, and I gather seeds for my jars. They improve the entrance to their nest, take out trash and debris, and I repair holes in irrigation pipes, rake leaves, clear and remove stones. The ants and I get up early, work in the cool hours of sunrise and sunset, and hide from the heat of the day—me in my home and they in theirs, and when the heat is unbearable I have also spotted them working in the middle of the night. I shine a flashlight on them in order to see, whereas they need no light at all.

In the winter, when I'm weeding, I never see them. They hunker down in closed nests until spring arrives and then, out of the blue, one hot day I suffer two or three small and familiar bites on my shins—and here they are: "Did you forget we live here, too? Did you think you'd never see us again? You're standing too close to our nest. Scoot off . . ."

They are right. I am the one who rudely invaded their space, and with each step I am likely to trample and stamp on them, to slaughter and slay. So I move away, and they resume their routine without further ado: the workers hasten to look for and fetch seeds, and the guards—it is easy to spot them because they are larger than their sisters and equipped with threatening jaws—either patrol close to the nest or accompany the workers. I wonder whether they are there to protect the workers or to ensure they are getting on with the job, like taskmasters of slaves in ancient history and overseers of day laborers today. Because this is the thing: in the ant society, the individual is valueless. The workers work, go out to the fields, harvest and bring food; the guards guard; the queen lays eggs; and the males fertilize. I see them once a year, on their nuptial night flight, when the garden fills with the radiance of their wings, attracting birds and lizards to come feast.

The life of the ant has clear, strict rules and regulations. They live in a totalitarian society that is also miraculously equal, because all members are slaves. It is doubtful they are aware of this, because their society is totalitarian to the extent that they have no need of coercive methods or threats. Even the queen ant, whom I have never seen, is enslaved to the general public. The title "queen" was given to her by humans, yet in spite of this description, she does not govern over the other ants in the nest. In fact, she is the most indentured slave: lying in the darkest depths of the nest laying more and more eggs that will create more and more workers, guards, and males.

The true sovereign here is not the queen but the genetics of the ant race governing the queen and all her offspring. It is genetics that condemns them to slavery and obedience, eradicating any individualism or rebelliousness. There is no room in this society for improvisation, compassion, variety, horseplay, criticism, curiosity, or creativity, and within the human heart this thing can arouse pity or admiration, identification or aversion—according to the beholder's opinions and personality.

The most famous admirer of ants was King Solomon, who praised them with his well-known words: "Go to the ant, thou sluggard, consider her ways and be wise: which having no guide, overseer or ruler, provideth her meat in the summer, [and] gathereth her food in the harvest." King Solomon's entomological curiosity and powers of scientific observation are to be praised, but it is difficult to ignore this fondness and appreciation of the ant society. More than any other biblical king of Israel, Solomon exploited the hard labor of his subjects for his own glorification, magnificence, and pleasure. More than any other king, he wanted his subjects to behave like ants.

"Go to the ant, thou sluggard, consider her ways and be wise," said the sluggard ruler, an idle hedonist who did not work a stitch his entire life: their crops and livestock became his meals, their sons and daughters became his slaves, and still he was jealous of the ant society that has no need for commissioners and overseers and oppressors because slavery is ingrained upon their very nature.

Other writers of fables like this pay heed to the industriousness of the ant. They praise it, preparing for a rainy day, and condemn the grasshopper—perhaps they really mean the cicada or the cricket—who spends summers in the garden and starves to death in winter. I am not sure that the grasshopper and the ant are themselves aware of the difference between them, but the fable was not written for them. We, the human race, have interpreted the behavior of these innocent insects for our own use. The most that can be said is that in each of us there is a grasshopper and an ant, and the powers that be prefer to reinforce the side of the ant.

I return to my garden: one of the ants' contributions to the appearance of the garden is the laying down of trails. From every nest of the harvest ant are several trails leading in various directions to various harvest fields. The length of these trails is between a few feet to tens of feet, and their breadth is three to four fingers wide. Millions of minuscule legs have conquered these trails, the same way the hooves of ibex and gazelles form trails in the desert, and the feet of shepherds and their flocks on mountainous slopes, and cloven hooves of wild boars in thickets. The pressure, the friction, the force of all the different types of feet on the ground for such a long time, displace stones and inhibit the growth of vegetation. A path is conquered, and the trail always possesses a logic that testifies to those who created it.

I like trails. In my childhood there were areas of uncultivated fields that stretched out between the Jerusalem neighborhoods. There were few cars and, in those days, people went from place to place on foot. The trails forged by their feet were clearly visible, and they had a beauty that also exists in quality tools and hand movements of veteran artisans: an economical beauty, indeed, tailored by purpose, usage, experience, and time. The ant trails, too, regardless of being conquered by minuscule legs, are formed by continuous and consecutive movement on the very same track, but there is something else that is unique to them. The ants go to their construction site and return from it to the nest. They do not deviate

from it, nor do they look right or left in order to pay a visit or to rest by the wayside or see the view and ruminate.

Indeed, the most prominent characteristic of ant trails is that they are devoid of junctions and bypasses. A crossroads is a place where there is a built-in choice, and a bypass can lead the ant to a different place, introduce it to other creatures and other ways of life and arouse forbidden thoughts within it, perhaps even doubt and uncertainty. But the ant is sentenced to imprisonment with hard labor; incarceration is embedded within its personality, devoid of choice, and its legs pave trails according to the needs of society and nest. In actual fact, any ant can abandon the trail at any given time. There are no fences lining its borders, but the fence is ingrained in its consciousness, its genetics, its essence, and the trail is not a trail of wandering or a commercial route, and definitely not a promenade or scenic route. It is a work trail, a path of drudgery and subjugation.

"A path of pain and a path of toil" is how Rachel the poet described the ant trail, adding:

> I know only to speak of myself,
> My world as narrow as an ant's.
> My load as much a burden,
> So heavy on my frail shoulders.

Here, Rachel the poet accurately pinpoints the ant's narrow existence, the hard labor, the toil and tribulations. She wrote a further poem about a trail, not formed by ants through hard labor and suffering, but one of her own:

> I did not sing to you, my land,
> Nor glorify your name
> With tales of heroes

Or battle trophies.
But my hands planted trees
By the tranquil Jordan
And my legs trod paths
Through your fields.

"Trod" is the original translation of the Hebrew *kavshu*, but other meanings have been ascribed to the root of this word, most notably "conquered," or *kibush* in Hebrew. Rachel emphasizes here that the path trod down by her feet does not subscribe to this meaning. This path of hers, and the tree she planted with her own hands, are the most beautiful gifts a person can offer the land, and they convey a completely different kind of connection to the land and a different sense of ownership.

10

Fruit Trees

A person who eats fruit from his own garden is generally considered to be a particularly happy person, but in spite of the romanticism of sitting under one's vine or fig tree, how much fruit can a person eat? And how many bursting and leaking bags of fruit can one thrust upon innocent guests? And how many jars of jam and preserves and compotes can one make, to distribute or store away? And let us not forget the extreme cases of orphans, widows, and widowers left with half a ton of jam by their dearly departed who planted too many fruit trees and added more jams and preserves to the overflowing collection of jars that they themselves inherited from a grandmother or an uncle who only wanted to sit under her or his plum or apricot tree and who finally drowned in a stewpot of jam or a cauldron of compote.

All this I saw, noted, and learned from: I did not plant many fruit trees in my garden, definitely not plums and apricots and apples and grapes, all of which yield a bountiful crop in a short amount of time, and many of which remain on the tree until they fall, attracting flies and wasps. Instead, I planted a few olive and pomegranate trees, fig and citrus, and left an old pear tree close by, planted long before my arrival. Its fruit is small and bland, but I love its springtime blooms.

The first fruit trees to be given names were the tree of life and the tree of knowledge that grew in the Garden of Eden. I would be happy to plant both these trees in my garden and to partake of their fruit, if only I knew which trees they were and where I could get hold of saplings for each of them. For now, I make do with the pleasurable knowledge that, according to the Bible, these two most important and coveted qualities—life and knowledge, which, according to the story, delineate the difference between good and evil—are actually derived from plants.

The first known tree was the fig tree, not because of its wonderful fruit but because of its leaves. Adam and Eve sewed themselves loincloths from these leaves, ashamed of their nakedness after eating from the tree of knowledge. I suppose they chose the fig tree because of its large leaves, similar in shape to the palm of a hand, but the writer of the story chose the fig for the sexuality that oozed from it, in the shape of its fruit, from the linguistic closeness in Hebrew between the name of the tree, *te'ena*, and the word *ta'ana*, which means sexual excitement and passion.

The two fruit trees mentioned after the fig are connected to the story of the Deluge. The first is the olive tree, whose leaf a dove delivered to Noah after the water receded and the ark came to a halt. The vine is mentioned after this, also connected to Noah but in a different way. Right after leaving the ark, Noah planted a vineyard, waited until it bore fruit—several years—made himself some wine, and got himself as drunk as Lot before Lot was even born. In fact, the word "grapevine" is not mentioned here, but since the words "vineyard" and "wine" are, there is no mistaking it.

Either way, the fig, vine, and olive, who enjoy neighborly relations throughout our area to this day, are a well-known and steadfast biblical trio. Sometimes only two of the three appear, for example: "They shall sit every man under his vine and under his fig" and "Thy wife shall be as a fruitful vine by the sides of thine house, thy children like olive plants round about thy table," and sometimes all three appear, such as in the parable of Jotham.

In this parable, the trees turned to the olive, the fig, and the vine with a proposal to reign over them. All three—aware of their worth and proud of their fruit and their contributions—rejected the proposal outright. This is another example of how the Bible does not favor politicians, preferring the leadership of God over a leadership of flesh and blood. But the agricultural aspect is actually more interesting: the first tree that was approached by the other trees, the one deemed worthy to rule, was the olive. This was not simply because of its splendor and power but due to its oil, whose importance in the life and nutrition of human beings was greater than that of figs and grapes. A sip of wine or the savoring of the first fig ahead of summer may pleasure the palate and please the heart, but olive oil provides real sustenance and a real existential need, life itself.

The olive has other qualities that stimulate empathy and appreciation: it is a distinct survivalist, able to revive itself after great trauma—fire, amputation, attacks from various pests, years of continuous drought. It is sturdy and lives for a long time, and does not cease producing fruit when old—a quality that human beings exalt and wish for themselves, not always successfully.

The olive trees I planted in my garden are growing nicely, and I hope that in a hundred or two hundred years' time, or even five hundred years' time, they will still be here and others will enjoy them. I am not an expert but try to look after them the best I can. Among other activities, I prune them according to a poetic rule I once heard: the olive tree should be pruned so that a bird can pass through it as it flies—in other words, the inner branches should be pared down to let air and light penetrate through to the landscape.

I must emphasize here that I planted the olive trees as young saplings. Not one of them was a large tree transplanted from one place to another, evidence of which can be seen in city squares and gardens of private homes today. The olive tree is easy to transplant, it acclimatizes well, and everyone has the right to buy and plant an olive tree like this in his or her garden, but it makes me uncomfortable, and sometimes I even chuckle when I see a stately olive tree in the garden of a newly constructed home: the plaster is still damp, the tiles glitter, the bushes are mere babies, but a graying octogenarian has already been positioned in the garden, as if planted by the very grandfather of the father of the person who owns the house—who in most cases has never held a hoe in his life. And, on occasion, the reason for my sense of unease is different, since not all these ancient trees arrived at their new abodes in an amicable or legal fashion.

As for the nonbiblical and less political trees in my garden, these are mostly citrus trees, which are highly suited to my needs and consumption. Their fruit lasts a long time on the tree, can be eaten or squeezed, consumed immediately or frozen. I have both pomelo and pomelit, lemon and lime, and also kumquats, but my tastiest citrus fruit is the blood orange.

Some people detest this orange. The red veins woven through it remind them of raw meat and the blush of its juice—the fluid by which it is named. I, on the other hand, am very happy when my blood oranges ripen. I either drink them or eat them—either way they are more delectable to my palate than any other citrus fruit.

I also squeeze the pomegranates and take delight not just in the taste but in the pleasant blow they give to the gut of whoever drinks their juice. But I love eating the separated seeds in a bowl. Deseeding the pomegran-

ate is an annoying and messy task but well worth the effort, and out of all the methods various experts have taught me, only one has proven itself: cut the pomegranate in quarters, fill a large, deep bowl or bucket with clean water, and remove the seeds while your hands and the pomegranate sections are immersed in water. The juice does not squirt, the seeds sink to the bottom, and the inner yellow pith floats to the surface. Collect and discard it then pour the water through a sieve, and you will have an impressive pile of seeds. By the way, drain the water into a pan or bucket, not the sink, and use it to water the pomegranate tree that gave you the fruit you just deseeded. The tree deserves it.

11

Home and Away

In Kenneth Grahame's *The Wind in the Willows* there are animals who
dwell happily at home. Badger, for example, lives in an underground
home with a bedroom and dining room and packed larders. In contrast
to such creatures, there are animals who are nomads and adventurers, like
Ratty, who sails all over the world and tells stories that leave his yearning
listeners in turmoil. Creatures like these are also present in nature itself:
the rat, the anteater, the rabbit, the bee, and the pigeon are all home dwellers. But the great herbivores are nomads.

Plants cannot wander around, and the possibility of moving from
place to place can only be realized by scattering their seeds. But not all
plants jump at the chance of doing this. There are plants that make a point
of distributing their seeds long distances, but others drop them directly to
the ground, creating large, overcrowded neighborhoods. The most prominent of these in my garden are annuals such as the lupines, the Syrian
cornflower-thistle, and the poppy and perennials such as the cyclamen,
the hyacinth squill, and the sea squill.

The sea squill, as I mentioned earlier, reproduces in two ways: above-
ground it produces seeds and then scatters them close by, and under-

ground it duplicates the bulbs. As a lover of squills I applaud this act of multiplication, since this is how the big squill kingdoms I love to walk in were formed, the same way in which squill colonies spread through my own garden.

The cyclamen sows its seeds within close proximity to itself. When I write "sow," I mean exactly that. Prior to its ripening, the cyclamen curls its capsules—the fruit which contains the seeds—downward, and even touches the ground, so that when the seeds open, they fall right beside it.

I recall reading somewhere that the cyclamen entrusts its seed distribution to ants. Although I have many ants and cyclamens in my garden, I have never seen any ants gathering around or helping themselves to seeds during the ripening season. Either way, the cyclamen's offspring grow close to their parents. Someone even made the comparison between plots of cyclamen and the kibbutz housing of long ago, in which the parents' homes, the children's houses, and the infant houses could all be seen, separate from one another and gradually spreading out.

I have tried to render the distribution policy of sea squills and cyclamens into words, and this is what these plants say: "If I manage to sprout and thrive, to develop bulbs and tubers that are sufficiently large, to blossom and make place for seeds, this is a sign that the place is a good and worthy habitat for my offspring." But in spite of the logic in what they are saying, there are plants that beg to differ. For example: "Don't put all your offspring in one basket" or "There might be a better place over the rainbow"—and they send their offspring far away. It is easy to succumb to the temptation of giving them human qualities such as adventurousness and bravado, a penchant for wanderlust and gambling, or simply a wish for a little peace and quiet after the young ones leave, but it is better to credit this to evolutionary considerations.

These plants even went to the trouble of developing methods of distribution that transport the seeds to great distances: types of wings, umbels, crests, and parachutes for flying in the wind, thistles and hooks for gripping the fur of animals or embedding in their skin, and also alluring taste substances and sources of energy, so that animals will eat the fruit and secrete the seeds elsewhere. The end result is that there are plants whose children remain with their parents, enjoying laundry facilities and free dinners, creating huge crowded clans, and there are plants that invest great effort in placing distance between themselves and their offspring.

This comparison between plants and human families has neither scientific backing nor meaning. It is merely an image and bears witness more to the man who likens himself to the plants he is describing. But plants

that disperse, the roaming ones—I once heard of a coconut whose fruit was tossed from side to side across the ocean waves, and which survived thousands of miles until landing on a different beach—these stir thoughts in the heart. I am not attributing human consciousness to plants, and it is obvious to me that humanizing them, which I am occasionally guilty of, has no basis. Their distribution mechanisms are the result of an evolutionary process and not an act with thought or program or future purpose behind it. But when ragwort or dandelion seeds fly above my garden, melting into the distance, they awaken within me a yearning and excitement coupled with anxiety for their fate. They make me think of great travelers and discoverers of new worlds, first people who sailed along the coastline and perhaps were swept out to sea and from there to a different place, and after that people who were not swept out to sea but who built rafts and carved oars, and perhaps hoisted masts and sails, and took with them seeds and plants and children, a gestating she-dog and pregnant sheep, and they sailed out to sea, hoping to arrive at a better place.

Why did they do that? Man has wanderlust and also curiosity and imagination, and various hardships may prompt him to uproot, but in order to set out on such a journey he needs either a hefty dose of bravery and optimism or a lack of choice and deep despair. All this is hard to attribute to plants, but even among plants there are both nomads and house dwellers, and you do not need to sail the seven seas in order to see them. It is enough to go out into this wild garden and to walk through it with open eyes.

12

Sabras

Once, every kibbutz had an old-timer who cultivated a cactus garden, and anyone who happened to be passing by was taken forcibly by the hand to this cactus garden to see cacti and hear stories about cacti and was even expected to enthuse over the grafting of cacti into all sorts of prickly monster shapes.

Regrettably, I am not that interested in cacti, but I do have one of my own, a cactus I am very fond of—a large sabra prickly pear that rises up at the rear of the garden. I did not plant it, nor do I look after it. From time to time I cut and remove creepers attempting to climb up its trunk to reach sun and light. Aside from that, I don't need to bother with it at all. It's a large, ancient creature, strong and independent, that survives in all conditions and overcomes all hardships. It does not need watering, either, since it hoards water in its succulent stems, and one is best advised not to touch it at all. It is possible, of course, but this is literally at the risk of those who choose to be in touch.

I do not know who planted this sabra. Perhaps the Arab tenants who lived in the area before it was purchased from its owner—a rich Arab who lived in Beirut—by Germans who established a village on it? Perhaps the Germans themselves, who decided to assimilate into the area? Or someone from the Israeli collective moshav that was established here after World War II, when the British expelled the Germans back over the seas? The sabra does not answer any of these questions but simply stands there, and every summer it blossoms and produces fruit that is good enough for me to eat.

Anyone hiking in Israel knows there are many sabra bushes like these, all looking as though they were sown by God in the middle of nowhere. Almost always, this nowhere was once an Arab village, but ironically the word "sabra" is a Zionist nickname for Jewish children who were born and raised here even before the establishment of the State of Israel, as is written in Eliezar Ben Yehuda's capacious dictionary: "A nickname for children raised in the Land of Israel who did not learn European manners." This can be understood in a positive light—a Hebrew child free of Diasporic complexes. And also in a negative light—an insolent and impolite Hebrew child.

There are varying claims as to the ownership of this innovative term, and I won't go into detail here. I will only say that it is customary to give the rather schmaltzy explanation that Israeli children are like the fruit of the sabra: prickly on the outside but soft and sweet on the inside. But the real reason, so I believe, goes a little deeper than this, namely that these bushes seemed to embody the essence of locality to new Jewish immigrants.

And indeed the poet Shaul Tchernichovsky in "Oh My Land, My Homeland" included the sabra among other quintessential local elements: goat herds, camel caravans (*gamelet,* to use his terminology), the scent of spring orchards, rocky ground, sycamores, and "a fence of wicked sabra"— something that brings to mind the possibility that the poet personally suffered a painful experience connected to this wickedness.

The Hebrew name *sabra* was derived from the Arabic *sabaar,* which was also granted the Yiddish declension of *sabrey*, or *sabreys* in the plural. But the shrub itself is neither Arab nor Jew, neither a Zionist nor an anti-Zionist, and the truth is it is not even indigenous. In spite of its successful branding, the sabra itself is not a sabra, born in Israel, but an immigrant. It is native Mexican, brought to Europe by the Spanish at the beginning of the sixteenth century. And because it acclimatized easily, and its fruit is so tasty, and its trunk can become an impassable obstacle, and also because it's a hardy plant that makes do with the bare minimum—it was joyfully adopted throughout the Mediterranean Basin, including Israel. While traveling, I have come across it in Sicily and Spain and Sardinia and France and Greece and Italy. I greet it each time the way one greets a relative or an acquaintance, and for a moment I feel at home.

On this note, by the way, the sabra is reminiscent of the eucalyptus—also a foreign plant that came from faraway Australia, acclimatizing here until it eventually turned into one of the scenic and political symbols of Israel. The eucalyptus can be seen in many areas of the Mediterranean, and wherever it grows, it provides shade, building rafters, and fuel for heating. It aids land conservation and the production of various medications and is used as a source of nectar and pollen for honeybees. In Israel, furthermore, the eucalyptus attained special status and was part of the Zionist enterprise and narrative, until the Arabs turned their attention toward it, nicknaming it "the Jew tree"—*shajarat el-yehud.*

Moreover, in a public opinion poll conducted by the Ministry of Agriculture, it was discovered that out of all the trees it is, in fact, the Australian immigrant that has gained the title of "the most Israeli tree of all." This is because the eucalyptus has been part of the Jewish settlement through all its variations and generations and has come to be identified with it. Like the sabra, the eucalyptus also benefited from a public relations campaign, from branding and image building: For years we were taught that the eucalyptus fought malaria alongside the pioneers, draining the swamps with them, dancing the hora with them, and spending time with female pioneers in the granary. In short, its image as a Zionist tree intensified and took root, like the tree itself. It accompanied many of us through our private lives, too—in the collective agricultural movement, in old established villages and kibbutzim, on hikes, in army camps, and along the numerous roads of Israel, thanks to its prominent presence within the landscape.

The sabra similarly accompanied those who were raised here—perhaps not many of today's children, but the fifty-plus group, without a doubt. In my Jerusalem childhood, I picked sabras in Lifta, Sheikh Badr, and on the western extension of Mount Herzl, also a former Arab village that has meanwhile been taken over by Yad Vashem. In my Nahalal childhood, I picked sabras at Ein Bedah, close to the Ramat David Air Base. The truth is I should have written "we picked," the plural, because we were always together, a barefoot troop of children, venturing out to pick sabras, like Tom Sawyer and Huckleberry Finn.

How does one pick them? Well, back then we would arm ourselves with a long stick to which an empty tin can was nailed at one end, wobbling like the milk tooth of a six-year-old. We chose fruit that was golden green—the ruddier colors are overripe—stretched the stick toward the fruit, inserted the tin can over it, tilted it, pulled, and if the can did not break loose and the fruit didn't fall, it was ours, complete with the minuscule, loathsome spines that quickly detach from the fruit and stick in your skin.

Today, a tin instrument made for this purpose can be purchased in any hardware store in the Arab villages of northern Israel. One side fits small sabras, and the other side fits large ones, and it also has a short tin sleeve that fits snugly and securely to the end of the stick, making it a very efficient and handy instrument. And there is another method, suitable for fruit within arm's reach: put a sturdy work glove on your hand, the cheapest and simplest type, grasp the fruit, and pick it. While picking sabras

with a stick or a glove, or any other method of picking, it is recommended to wear a long-sleeved shirt and to consider the direction in which the wind is blowing, because the spines break away and fly off, and to realize that all this will be in vain, that sabras are procured through suffering, although beyond their spines awaits the sweetness of the fruit.

You pick, you get pricked, you roll the harvested sabras on the ground, you get pricked some more, you strike them lightly with pine branches— the devout, so I've heard, do this with branches of sticky yellowheads— you get pricked again, drop them in a pail, go home, and try to remember not to wipe the sweat from your face, because that will become covered with spines, too. At home, wash the fruit under running water and then peel: with a sharp knife remove both ends of the fruit, make a cut from its North to South Pole, grasp either edge of the incision, get pricked again, and pull apart. If the incision is not sufficiently deep, the skin will tear and remain on the fruit. If it is too deep—the fruit will disintegrate. If it is sliced correctly, the fruit will peel with the ease of a man removing his coat. Taste, enjoy, and then discover that from this moment your tongue is also full of spines, and furthermore your inner cheek and palate, but the taste makes up for the suffering.

Now is the time for all sorts of people to arrive, asking for a taste. You might grumble: "Pick them yourself," but it is nicer to feed whoever is hungry, even if they are parasites who did not work hard, who did not pick or clean or get pricked. In any case, the sabras must be chilled before eating. Place them in the refrigerator and meanwhile ask a close friend, preferably the Dulcinea for whom you went out to pick sabras in the first place, to equip herself with a pair of tweezers in order to nitpick the spines from your skin.

And so, while the peeled sabras are cooling, stretch out on the cold floor and cool yourself as well, and while your beloved is attending to your wounds, rest on your laurels. Close your eyes and feel your forgotten manhood reawakening: here you are, the manliest among men, out hunting the most dangerous creatures in nature. Solo, with only a stick in hand, facing a gang of bandits armed with ten thousand minuscule burning spears and thousands of invisible daggers. Neither afraid nor withdrawing, stabbed yet vanquishing, picking and peeling, returning from the battle carrying an offering to the beloved—like David to Michal with two hundred foreskins in his basket.

Dear men, hear my voice; suitors and lovers, give ear to the words of my mouth: pick sabras for your loved ones, as I did for mine. The sabra is a vegetarian dish, organic, valiant, and manly, yet not crude or violent, nor chauvinistic. Pick sabras, peel them, place them in the refrigerator, and in the heat of the day welcome your loved ones with this oh-so-sweet chilled delight. Enough of "I squeezed you a glass of wheatgrass, my dove." From henceforth say: "I picked you a sabra. Do you want it?"

And you, dear lady reader, even if that very day you went to the supermarket and bought a cellophane-wrapped tray of sterile, tasteless, and odorless sabras, polite ones devoid of spines from the outset, wrap your arms around your Ulysses and draw him toward you—just as at the end of the book of the same name—drawn to your perfume and your breasts, and his heart will beat like mad, and you will say: "You picked sabras for me? Yes, I want them . . . yes I will Yes."

13

Seasons

Whenever I travel abroad, the moment arrives—after about two and a half days—in which I become homesick. What causes this? I must admit that I do very well without some inherently Israeli features like cottage cheese, news bulletins, the practice of passing on the hard shoulder, soup mandels, friendly slaps, and Turkish coffee, and with a bit of effort I even manage to overcome the distance from Joseph's tomb, his mother's tomb, also his father's, grandmother's, and grandfather's. I miss a few loved ones, my home, my wild plants, the Hebrew language, and a few landscapes.

Not that many landscapes, since most countries I have visited offer more beautiful ones than those in Israel. The Mediterranean beaches of Italy, Turkey, Greece, and Spain, for example, are more beautiful than ours, their trees and mountains are higher and their waters more exuberant, but their landscapes do not offer me memories and histories, and there is something else here at home that these foreign landscapes lack: a wide variety of weather and types of soil, and the possibility of moving from forest to desert within two to three hours, from snow to sand, from considerably high to the lowest of the low. We also have a huge number of plants, relative to such a small territory, many more than in larger countries, and also fascinating next-door neighbors: it is only in Israel that I have seen oak and acacia trees growing together, or broom and carob, because we are located at the crossroads of three continents.

The real problem, however, begins when I travel beyond the Mediterranean to countries where I miss something else—our changing seasons. With all my enthusiasm for the Indian summers of Vermont, the longest day of the year in Nordkapp, Norway, and the inverted seasons of Australia and South Africa, I am accustomed to and in need of the Mediterranean cycle of seasons: winter, spring, summer, and fall, each one with its own scents and sights and sounds, and the differences between them.

And also the way in which these seasons change: not all at once but gradually, in the close-by garden and faraway landscape. Anyone whose body is responsive and who remembers, whose skin knows the various touches of air, whose ears recognize sounds, those that come down from the heavens and those that rise up from the weeds and those that are insinuated from within the thicket, whose eyes predict the changing colors in forest foliage and whose nose recognizes scents—this person also knows that somehow the struggle between seasons steadily weakens at the decisive moment, and it does not end in the victory of the victor but in capitulation of the defeated. Neither with fanfares of victory of the one, nor in the rasping death of the other, but in a slow withdrawal and eventual disappearance that says: We'll be back.

After the Deluge, God promised mankind: "While the earth remaineth, seedtime and harvest, and cold and heat, and summer and winter, and day and night shall not cease"—meaning that world order, its times and seasons, will never again be breached. Aside from "seedtime" and "harvest," the phenomena and changes described here are all part of the natural order. But it is a bit more complicated. "Seedtime" and "harvest" are words denoting agricultural activities, whereas here they are used as synonyms for "autumn" and "spring" and are not referred to by their precise names, as summer and winter are. It appears that the writer wanted to express the connection between people, their lives and work, and nature, its appointed times and seasons.

Some climate experts claim that there are not four but only two seasons in our region, summer and winter. What we call autumn and spring are but the frontlines and the no-man's-land that lies between them. Some linguists have determined that *stav,* or "autumn," is the correct Hebrew name for the rainy season, which today we refer to as "winter," as it is written: "For, lo, the autumn is past, the rain is over and gone." In my opinion, this sentence can be read literally, meaning that two seasons have passed, one after the other: first autumn and then winter, but even from the perspective of how the year is divided I cannot accept this concept. The period of time between summer and winter is not as clearly demarcated as record low temperatures, January precipitation, or the heavy heat of August, but still it has its own character and attributes—in plants, animals, weather, agriculture, and our own physical and mental feelings.

The word "summer" in Hebrew, *kayitz,* is related to the word *ketz,* which means "end." Is it possible to reach the conclusion that Hebrew sees summer as the end of the year? Every point on a circle can be perceived as both a beginning and an end, but this is not so with regard to the cycle of seasons in Israel. Flowering, for example, begins midwinter, continues through spring until almost the middle of summer, but in autumn the flowering virtually disappears, the majority of plants wither, and in a regular rainy season, a new cycle of life is already germinating at autumn's end. Consequently, autumn can be perceived as a season that is both an ending and a beginning.

It is the same with agriculture, too, because autumn is a season of harvesting the fruits of the year gone by and sowing the year that is to come. Those who are so inclined will say that it is not merely an agricultural harvesting but a spiritual one. Regrettably, I am not the spiritual type, but even so I notice the influence of autumn on body and soul. The grass withereth, the flower fadeth, with not even one blossom in sight, save for the first meadow saffron and the last sea squill and, if you are lucky or know where to look, also sternbergia or lilies and perhaps even a first crocus, but the general impression is one of a wasteland, even with regard to fruit trees: the joy of the prickly pear and fig has passed, there are few gleanings in the vineyard, the citrus has not yet ripened, and only the last few pomegranates remain to pleasure the eye and the palate. The forest sheds its leaves and dapples into gray, clouds stain azure skies, and even flocks of migrating birds that fill me with happiness in springtime now sadden the heart.

This is when farmers grow concerned—will it rain or not? Their concern burgeons into soul-searching and remorse. For many people, drought is seen as a punishment for those who have not fulfilled God's commandments. But there are also the city dwellers, and they can afford a more poetic response. Anyone who wants to look the part and is in the mood can tie a scarf around his or her neck, walk along the city streets, observe yellow leaves swirling around in the wind, and be overcome by a sweet "What is this life if, full of care" sadness. This same person may seek the intimacy of a sad and sensitive kindred soul with whom to celebrate gloom in all its sweetness and perhaps share warmth on the threshold of a chilly winter. As for my own autumnal gloom, this is born of the shortening of daylight hours, and the beloved can be searched for in other seasons. Why must the lover be limited to autumn? One can be romantic in summer, spring, and winter, too.

A s I mentioned earlier, my house faces a natural forest that stretches out, and within which the seasons shift their colors. The majority of the trees are gall oak and terebinth, and in autumn their leaves turn yellow and drop to the ground, and the forest is taken over by the gray of their bare branches. The verdant patches that remain in it are trees that do not shed their leaves: the Palestine oak, the mastic tree, and here and there a carob. In springtime the gall oak resumes its leafing. In their first days the leaves are pale green, both intense and subdued at the same time, and the terebinth lends a reddish hue to the forest. The entire forest swiftly turns green in all its variations, until eventually summer raises dust, and everything becomes a different green, a muted one. The first rains wash the leaves, and the forest begins to gleam again, and then autumn arrives, and so on and so forth.

The same goes for the fields opposite my house, their colors changing with beautiful regularity, but the fields are dependent not only on nature but also farmers. The green arable land is reaped and then yellows, and sometimes the land is yellow before it is reaped, and the yellow turns dusty brown, and later into the rich and deep brown of postplowing, and then the green sprouts forth, captivating the fields anew. Those acquainted with this can tell the month of the year according to the color of the field, but while the Hebrew language uses numbers to classify the hours as well as the days of the week, excepting the Sabbath—it gives names to the months of the year, and because these names originated in foreign languages, they mean nothing to us at all.

The truth is that the names of the months in Hebrew are actually foreign names with obscure meanings. Which Hebrew speakers know the meaning of Tishrei, Tavet, Marcheshvan, and Elul? There is a certain grace to these names, and some of them are truly beautiful, like Adar, Tamuz, and Iyar, but it is important to set the record straight: the names of the months that are referred to as "Hebrew" came to us from other languages and cultures, just like "July," "November," and "April."

Most worthy of the title of "Hebrew calendar" is that of the Gezer

tablet, named after the place in which it was first discovered. It is an agricultural calendar, within which are written the names of moons—lunar months—that are no longer in use: two moons of gathering, two moons of planting, two of late sowing, a moon of cutting flax, of reaping barley, of reaping and measuring grain, two moons of pruning, and a single moon of summer fruit.

Not every scholar agrees on the meaning of these names, but without a doubt they all signify agricultural activities: reaping and harvesting, sowing and sprouting, pruning and picking. Today it is too late to reintroduce this calendar, but it is nice to know that months like these once existed, not grand names of Roman or Mesopotamian gods and rulers, but concepts taken from the everyday working life of this country, some of which still exist within the Hebrew language.

Today, Israeli agriculture is no longer high on the list of priorities either of society or government and with new crops and modern methods is no longer faithful to the order of the Gezer tablet. Many crops grow and ripen year-round. Crops that were unknown during biblical times grow here today, while others were abandoned and have disappeared. But for those familiar with it, nature still serves as a calendar and a clock, as does the wild garden, which shows me both cyclical and linear time.

Anyone attentive to the sounds from within the garden and its changing hues and scents—whose feet have touched the soil and whose skin has sensed the heat of the sun's rays, the wind's caress, and the burr's prick—will also know its seasons. Just as everyone knows the sun rises in the morning and the moon at night, there are those who know which flower begins blossoming in which month and, waking at dawn, they know what time it is according to which bird is singing. For me, personally, there is another sign—the place where the sun sets over the Carmel mountain range, a place that changes throughout the year. In summer, the sunsets move across the mountain range from south to north and in winter from north to south. Since the railings of my balcony similarly stretch from south to north, I am considering marking on them the place where the sun sets every week, thereby relinquishing the need for not only a clock but also a calendar.

As an extension of nature, the garden is an analogical clock. It has hands that move in a circle: the small hand of big time, the hand of years and their seasons; and the large hand of small time, the hand of the hours of a day. Both are not only visible to the eye but heard by the ear and smelled by the nose. The hands of the garden demarcate this in the blossoming and sprouting and withering of its plants, in the mud and cracks and dust of its earth, in the mating calls and possessiveness of the tufted titmouse and the cooing of turtledoves and hooting of scops owls and the buzzing of bees, and the crevices out of which snails crawl.

The small hand of this seasonal calendar indicates the end of summer with the songs of the last cicadas and the warm scent of dust that our feet and the wind raise from the ground. It says "autumn" in the sounds that invisible cranes send down from the firmament, it announces midsummer with the hoarse screeching of adolescent jaybirds whose colors, daring, and size are as great as the number of days since their hatching. The big hand shows the hour of the day, and this does not just mean the rising of the sun in the morning or its setting at night. It is also the afternoon's western wind and the cries of the stone curlews announcing that dawn is here.

The terebinth tree's shadow, its size, direction, and coolness, tell me it is nine in the morning, the red leaflets of the pomegranate herald the beginning of March, and the size of the squill leaves at the bottom of the slope reminds me that I planted them years ago, just as my skin and hair reveal my own age. And because we are talking about me and my garden here, the significance is that in a few years' time I will still sow squills here, but will never see them blossoming.

14

Weeding

Every year, particularly at the end of winter and spring, I spend many hours on my knees. This is no display of supplication or begging for surrender, nor is it a dramatization of "he'll come crawling back on all fours" and other such salutations and orations concerned with humiliation and inferiority. All these are derived from the lowliness of a man on bended knees, and the fact that walking on all fours belongs to beasts and animals, whereas the human—superior in his own eyes—stands erect and walks on two legs. But I willingly crawl on all fours for my own benefit, and I do so because I find this a comfortable way to tend the weeds that grow in my garden. I have a pair of old and worn-out trousers for this purpose, with soil embedded in the knees that never disappears when soaked or scrubbed or washed.

Weeding, *isuv* in Hebrew—veteran farmers pronounce the final letter as a hard *b* rather than the more usual soft *v*—is an extremely important craft. It begins in winter, when weeds sprout, and continues as they grow, and is carried out mostly toward spring and up until it ends, because this is the last opportunity to get rid of the weeds before they produce seeds that will sprout the following year.

And why do I carry out this extremely important job on all fours? "Because after all I'm an elderly lady," as my grandmother used to tell everyone, and once again I have no choice. Young and agile gardeners do their weeding bent over. Elderly gardeners stoop down but rest one arm on a knee or sit on a stool or hire a gardener. I decided to get down on my knees, and this is why I am numbered among the family of weeders on all fours.

The weeds in my garden possess a strength and vitality that no other plants have, not only in comparison with domesticated plants, but also in comparison with the wild plants I grow. The calendula in my garden, for example, is hardy and spreads much farther than the cornflower, and the reason is simple: one I am interested in; the other I am not. If I were to switch preferences, the calendula would immediately weaken, and the cornflower would take over the garden and threaten to cover it completely.

Regarding these observations, Rabbi Hanina ben Pazzi preceded me when he said, "These thorns are neither weeded nor sown, yet of their own accord they grow and spring up, whereas how much pain and toil is required before wheat can be made to grow." These words appear in Genesis Rabba as an allegory for the easy impregnation of Hagar and the daughters of Lot. They and their sons—Ishmael, Moab, and Ammon— were comparable in Rabbi Hanina ben Pazzi's eyes to thorns that multiply and flourish although they are not sown, the area around them is not weeded, and they are not cared for, as compared with our four outstand- ing matriarchs, likened to wheat, who suffered and exerted themselves in order to conceive. I will add something else from the Bible to this: the Israelites in Egypt multiplied and grew the more they were afflicted and persecuted, exactly like the thorns and weeds in my garden, which sprout and grow and multiply sevenfold.

Rabbi Hanina ben Pazzi's lesson suggests a particular arrogance over other nations that is recognized and known within other nations and cultures, too. But within this allegory the simple despair of a cultivator of the land, battling weeds unsuccessfully, is considerable. I should know: year after year, I crawl on all fours in the mud, weeding and tearing out and uprooting, utterly overthrowing the enemy exactly as I overthrew and eradicated it from the face of the earth last year, and I will continue annihilating the enemy once and for all in years to come. In doing this, I think not only about myself but about all our other annihilators and exterminators and liquidators, although they, as compared with myself, stand tall and will not prostrate themselves or bow down, whereas I acknowledge the real ratio of power and crawl on all fours.

Not that solutions are lacking. Things have changed since the days of Rabbi Hanina ben Pazzi, agriculture has progressed, and today farmers spray weeds with all kinds of poison and weed inhibitors. But these substances are powerful and dangerous, and my garden is no modern agricultural field. It is a nature reserve, not just because of the various plants that grow there but because of the methods I use. Furthermore, it is a fraction of the size of huge wheat or corn or vegetable fields, and spraying it might damage the plants I grow and value, and, of course, spraying pollutes the ground.

For this reason, I have tried and am still trying various other methods: I till the enemy when it begins to sprout—but this is not sufficient. I cover sections of the garden with nylon sheeting—but it is not a pleasant sight to behold. I cut the weeds with a power scythe, and although it works very efficiently under certain conditions, it doesn't pull out the enemy by its roots, and due to its incredible speed it also cuts plants I do not want to eliminate. Once I even considered hiring a gardener or a laborer, but I was sure that my buttercups and cyclamens would not take kindly to this. In short, there is no choice. A land invasion is required, a close-quarters battle on planted territory from terrace to terrace and from flower bed to flower bed. Face-to-face combat at point-blank range, to see the green of its eyes, to grasp it by the neck and root it out. This is the only way to win, annihilate, and eradicate, until the next extermination campaign the following winter.

The weeding is continuous, monotonous, slow, and boring. Through the years I have also acquired the ability to easily distinguish between "for us" and "for our adversaries" in the garden, and therefore the battle of the weeds no longer requires my attention or singular thought. And since the human brain does not like to be idle, passing deliberations creep into the heart: about man and land, about what the land gives and what it covers and conceals, about living on the land and the respite within it, about all the blood and the brothers crying from within me and within the land, all that has happened until now and all that will follow, and to what purpose and just because and otherwise and why.

This is why the actual act of crawling on all fours also helps, returning me to early evolutionary stages and debates. My body fills with arguments. I hear my knees begging to return to an upright position, and my spine vigorously objecting, declaring that as far as it is concerned, I can stay in this position forever, and it even tries to convince my skin that it can go back to sprouting fur. I feel my fingers, rummaging among the plants, grasping stems and encountering roots and bugs, fingers that in days gone by foraged for food. Indeed, I take this opportunity to gather wild spinach and chicory, from which a side dish can be made for a meal.

Crawling on all fours also affords an alternative perspective and agreeable sense of humility. It brings the nose and the eye and the ear closer to buds that usually remain unseen, and also the little creatures that live among them: various kinds of lizards and spiders and earthworms and insects and skinks that bustle around there, particularly in springtime, escaping the hand that pulls out the plants under which they hide, revealing to me that my world is one of a myriad of worlds existing side by side in this little universe—right here in my garden.

Wonder creeps into the heart: Whom, in fact, am I fighting here? Why and for what? Surely all the plants I grow, and also the plants I root out, are wild ones. If this is so, who decides that buttercups are preferable over clover? And what does squill have over ragwort? And blue cornflower over thistle? And hollyhock over mallow? Perhaps I've become afflicted with the inclination of certain environmental and nature conservation organizations to stand up for dolphins and pandas rather than toads and spiders?

There are gardeners of wild areas with principles and commandments. They do not meddle with the natural processes that exist in their gardens. They will not weed or sow or water or fertilize. But my garden and I are less ideological, and religiosity in any sphere is repugnant to me. I prefer cyclamens to briars, although both are wildflowers, and I intervene in the struggle for survival that prevails in the garden, weeding those I do not desire and giving an unfair advantage to those I cherish. During droughts and particularly severe heat waves I even water my flowers a little, pruning the shoots that the Judas tree and bay laurel produce around the trunk and shaping the carob, so that one day I will be able to sit in its shade with friends. For the exact same reasons, I also gather up and store and sow the seeds in better and safer conditions than those provided by nature.

Added to this is the human inclination, common also to those who are close to nature and who love it, to see weeding as a battle between good and evil, like a civilized person battling barbarians, or Gideon against the Midianites. Connected to this is an interesting phenomenon: all the wild plants I sow and plant and grow and love are ones that I know personally, each one by name and appearance, according to both its general shape and each of its parts at every stage of its life. But the enemies, the same endless moblike pack of wild plants that I declare war on, they are all one solid mass in my mind and have no names. They are "crabgrass" and "bad weeds" and that's it. The eye recognizes them and the hand is skilled at pulling them out, but apart from an incensed, general "know thine enemy," there is nothing between us at all.

As a matter of fact, I know one of them close-up, and actually it is one I find particularly annoying: it has a pale root that resembles parsley but slenderer and more delicate, and its stems, which bear serrated leaves, are close to the ground. The power scythe fails to cut it and fingers have trouble getting hold of the stem and pulling it out by the roots.

Toward the end of its life this plant changes from green to pale blue-gray, its stem stands tall, hardens, and produces small thorny fruits which stick to socks, trousers, or fur—depending what one has on one's shins. I went to the trouble of finding out that the name of this bad pest is *gzir,* known in English as spreading hedge parsley or tall sock-destroyer, and botanists here even refer to it as "*gazir* pest," as if wanting to give reason and validation for my feelings.

Over the years, the crabgrass and I have reached a certain balance of terror. But there are surprises within it, too, and the last word has yet to be spoken. When I arrived here, the house was surrounded by nettles and calendulas. I wanted to eradicate the nettles entirely, and the calendulas—a nice-looking plant but one that tends to occupy and settle—I wanted to whittle down. So after a few years of my systematic weeding and mowing, the garden was once again devoid of even a single nettle, and the calendulas retreated to the area I allocated to them.

I naïvely thought I had succeeded. Here and there, when friends or colleagues who also enjoy gardening told me that the battle of crabgrass is a lost one, I offered the nettles and calendulas as proof that it is possible to triumph over them. But a few more years passed, and one winter—I remember the astonishment that gripped me—I suddenly discovered a carpet of nettles in a part of the garden that had never suffered from them, and the calendulas returned, swiftly spreading over extensive areas.

If I were paranoid, this would have convinced me that some adversary

or enemy had secretly sown them for reasons known to him alone. But the truth is that nature has her own ways of teaching us humility. This is why I buckled up my dirty old work trousers, got down on my knees, and returned to battle. A wild garden needs to preserve boundaries and laws, and love for that garden requires investment and effort. This is exactly what should be done in other spheres and interests of life, if you want flowers to bloom there.

15

Big Trees

I once visited the Cambridge University Botanic Garden in England. As is customary in botanic gardens and zoos, a huge banner hung at the entrance. Botanic and zoological gardens usually display photos of orchids or cute pandas, but it was a picture of a thistle that was on show. A simple thistle. A nondescript Mediterranean thistle, which, in our parts, thrives in scrubland and on neglected plots and is swiftly uprooted when it grows in people's gardens. The botanic garden in Cambridge, however, is a scientific garden, and science respects all plants equally.

We in the Middle East have contributed not only thistles to the Cambridge University Botanic Garden but also white-leaved savory and rue, thyme, and sage and hyssop and all types of lavender, and they all appear in a large Mediterranean flower bed called the Scented Garden, because its plants surprise and enchant the British snout that is unaccustomed to such grace. But the plant which thrilled me the most was an entirely different comrade from all the others detailed here—a tremendous plant, a huge one, the biggest tree in our region: the cedar of Lebanon.

I like big trees. On my first visit to the United States I rushed off to see the parks of California, to see the sequoia trees and the redwood. In Giardino Garibaldi in Palermo I saw two Bengal ficus trees, which in spite of being pruned are huge and fill the heart with happiness. Once, on a hike in Western Australia, I climbed to the crown of the Gloucester Tree, a eucalyptus of the karri type. This tree is two hundred and thirty-six feet high! To the side of its trunk are steel rungs that can be climbed in stages, like a ladder, and at the top is a small platform. I climbed it and stood there, swaying in the wind above the entire forest, incredulous. I felt like the scout at the top of a flagpole out at sea. I was sure that any moment a whale would appear, blowing between the waves of green treetops like Moby-Dick.

Size also enables me to carry out amateur botanic classifications. In addition to the features according to which trees are classified—ornamental and fruit trees, deciduous and nondeciduous, monoecious and dioecious, wild and domesticated trees—I give them another marker: big trees and all the rest.

How can a tree's size be determined? By height? Diameter of the trunk? Circumference of the treetop? None of these provides a definitive or decisive criterion, but when you see a big tree you know it is just that, and you hear it, too: the wind rustling through the branches is more pleasurable and varies from the gusts of wind that blow through the branches of its smaller brothers. You feel it, too: all plants emit oxygen, vigor, and assorted fragrances, but large trees also emit calmness and security and a pleasant sense of boundless fascination. Large animals similarly inspire awe and wonderment. They also inspire fear, which trees do not.

I am neither the first nor the last to love big trees. The Greek historian Herodotus described in his writings a meeting between Xerxes, king of Persia, and a tree like this. At the time, Xerxes was marching to war with Greece, and on his way from Phrygia to Lydia, in what is Turkey today, he spied an enormous tree that entranced and amazed him with its beauty and dimensions. He decked out the tree with gold ornaments and appointed an immortal guardian to watch over it.

Xerxes was Khshayarsha, sometimes identified with Ahasuerus, from the Book of Esther. This big tree, which in Hebrew is *armon,* or "chestnut," was translated into English as the plane tree. It seems the English translation identifies it correctly, because this tree is extremely large. It grows in Israel as well, but in Turkey it reaches an even greater size. This tree, and no other, also appears in Handel's opera, *Xerxes,* in the aria "Ombra Mai Fu." The meaning of these words is "never was a shade like this," and the aria describes the beloved shade of this plane tree, unrivalled in its beauty and delightfulness, and expresses a wish that the tree remain undamaged by fate, thunder, lightning, and storms.

By the way, people wishing to see a really huge plane tree should treat themselves to a trip to the village of Tsagarada on the half island of Pelion, north of Athens. In the center of many Greek villages there is a large plane tree, or even several, in whose shade one can sit, eating and drinking and conversing with friends. But the plane tree of Tsagarada is really the most impressive of all. I went there and, upon seeing it, I understood why Xerxes was so moved by his own plane tree.

Whatever name the tree is given, and whatever name he is known by— Khshayarsha, Xerxes, Serse, or Ahasuerus—its story contains the seed of a promising plot. When reading Herodotus's writings for the first time I tried to imagine the guard chosen to watch over this tree. Who was he? And what is the meaning of the title "immortal guardian" that he was given? There was an elite unit in the Persian army whose warriors were known as the immortals, and it is possible that the guard was part of this unit. This does not, however, solve the problems involved in this kind of guarding.

If the word "immortal" indicates that the guard was endowed with supernatural qualities, then some of these problems can be explained, but it hurts the literary qualities of what Herodotus wrote. I, for example, prefer to describe him as a mere mortal, made immortal by the very fact of guarding the tree, because the plane tree can live for hundreds of years and perhaps infused this quality into the guard as well.

Either way, the massive Persian army continued west, and the lone warrior remained behind, close to the tree that amazed the king so much that he imposed this cruel and arbitrary mission upon the warrior. The reader, who continues moving along with the Persian army, asks himself: What happened to the guard in the days that followed? The months? The years? Who supplied the guard with food and drink? What did he do when his eyes closed and he needed sleep? Who protected him from other people and fierce animals? Who looked after him when he was sick? And what kind of a relationship developed between guard and tree? Between the guard and the people living close by? Did a man, or a woman, keep him company? Was he a disciplined soldier who watched over the tree until the day he died, or did he abandon his post and return home? Did he hang himself from one of the branches? Or perhaps, overcome with anger and loneliness, did he chop down the tree?

Did Xerxes ask himself these questions? And the guard's fellow soldiers? The large Persian army suffered a heavy defeat in the war against the Greeks. The soldiers returned home, and Herodotus does not say whether or not the guard rejoined them. Perhaps he was forgotten by his king and countrymen? In either case, the image of a lone soldier guarding a massive tree far from home is a seed full of potential, literary or cinematic.

Our country is not blessed with really big trees. It is true we do have a few large tamarisk trees, majestic Atlantic terebinths, and sizable carobs, but our biggest oak trees are small in comparison with average oak trees in Europe, the treetops of our plane and hackberry trees merely chaff the ankles of their Turkish cousins, and in Kenya I saw acacia trees whose shade can host four of our Hebrew acacias at once. All this is generously compensated for by the cedar of Lebanon. As its name suggests, this is not a native Israeli tree, but it is all right to be proud of the neighbor's trees as well, particularly when this neighbor is so large and magnificent.

That visit to the botanic gardens in Cambridge was not the first time I had ever seen a cedar tree. I also saw it in its natural habitat, and my breath was taken away by the sight. It is not as tall as other conifers: the sequoia and redwood I came across in the United States and the karri tree I climbed in Australia are all taller than the cedar, but its spreading branches create a fantastic silhouette, far more impressive than those huge, thick-trunked, towering trees.

In the language of biblical Hebrew—in spite of the fact that the majority of its users had never seen a live cedar tree but rather polished rafters of Solomon's temple and palace—the cedar itself symbolizes might and splendor. Incidentally, it is interesting to note that the palace Solomon built for himself was far bigger than the temple he built for his God. Perhaps this was because Solomon had a thousand wives, whereas God, whom we sentenced to solitude and celibacy in the form of monotheism, has not even one. But to return to the subject at hand: The verses "From the cedar tree that *is* in Lebanon even unto the hyssop that springeth out of the wall" and "If a flame among the cedars falls, what avails the lichen on the wall?" and "whose height was that of the cedar and who was as strong as the oaks." Since I already mentioned the picture of the thistle at the entrance to the Cambridge University Botanic Garden, I will also mention that Jehoash, king of Israel, joined the thistle and cedar together in one verse in order to ridicule Amatziah, the king of Judah, who sought to battle against him: "The thistle that was in Lebanon sent to the cedar that was in Lebanon, saying, give thy daughter to my son to wife: and there passed a wild beast that was in Lebanon, and trod down the thistle."

Regretfully, the cedar has disappeared from the thesaurus of similes and idioms of modern Hebrew. Folks from my parents' generation, of course, still used the term "solid as a cedar," but even that well-known expression in Israel has faded away. And as for thistles and thorns, they have also lost standing among proverbs and idioms. In Hebrew we no longer say "a fat tail with a thorn in it" but only "a thorn in the butt." That's it. I dare to suggest the unlikelihood that the good people of Cambridge know all this, but it is of little consolation to me: they have a cedar growing in their garden; I have none.

16

A Night in the Garden

I have written here of the big old pear tree in the garden, whose blossoms are lovely but whose fruit is inedible. The time has come to admit that this is my own opinion, and there are others who really love the taste: once a year a colony of fruit bats descends upon the garden, and they, unlike me, have no interest in pear blossoms but are partial to the fruit and come to gorge themselves. The pear tree stands close to the house, and as soon as they appear I rush to the balcony, sit down, switch on the light, and use a bright flashlight in order to watch them lunging toward their nighttime feast.

These bats are not permanent fixtures in my garden. They come from afar, perhaps from the Carmel caves, for only one or two nights in the year, when the fruit ripens. Their visit is a unique and wondrous spectacle, different from any other spectacle offered by the garden. Since I also know how to identify ripe pears, I prepare myself for these flying dinner guests: incline my ear, peer into the dark—Are they here? Not yet? And I wonder, How do they know it is time? Do they send scouts and spies? How do they navigate through the darkness to the specific coordinate of a tree? Do they remember the route from previous years? Either way, I am happy at their arrival, because they cast an atmosphere of authentic savagery and wildness over my garden.

Although they are vegetarians, bats possess a predatory quality. They are large, nimble, and noiseless. They lunge at the fruit-laden tree like birds of prey. Each time a bat dives, it collects a pear and carries it to the nearby oak to consume it. I suppose this habit is designed to avoid over-crowding, collisions, and squabbles on the tree itself and to enable each bat to eat undisturbed, but I have no way of corroborating this hypothesis. I sit and watch them for hours and eventually thank them and say good night, and the next morning there are neither bats nor pears, and the garden resumes a restful pose until the bats return the following year.

Porcupines are additional nocturnal visitors to my garden. I have never seen them here, but sometimes they leave traces of digging, a few black-and-white quills, and easily identifiable droppings. Here and there I see hedgehogs, endearing creatures I like a lot and who, I am sorry to say, visit infrequently and are becoming increasingly rare. On summer nights, jackals and wild boars also venture into the garden. These are real pests, who have learned to dig up irrigation pipes to quench their thirst by biting into them. The wild boars also cause alarm. I was once forced to stand on my germination table after suddenly hearing the furious snorting of a female arriving with her offspring and already planning to charge at me. We stood facing each other for some minutes, me on the table and she on the ground. We cursed, snorted, spoke without mincing our words, and were generally boorish to each other. Finally, she came to the conclusion that I am a bad role model for her children. She called to them, and took off.

Nighttime is the kingdom of sound, and most nocturnal occurrences are detected aurally. Darkness descends with the blackbird's final calls and continues with the jackal's yelping, sometimes very close to home. The jackals come back much later to yelp some more, and occasionally return for a midnight encore. In my humble opinion, this is how the packs tell one another where they are in order not to waste time and energy on arguments and skirmishes. I am certain of this because I already understand some of their words, and others I infer. This is how I translate some of their nightly exchanges:

"We're at the dumpster tonight. How about you?"

"We're down at the chicken coop on the kibbutz."

"Howww . . . Howwww . . . did you manage to get inside?"

"That's a secret."

And sometimes I hear the jackals when the muezzin from the nearby village calls, and they join in. All this is good. They are God's creatures, too, and were created by His will and His word, and they also have the right to supplicate and to jack up God's glory. Who knows, perhaps "jackal" and "jack" share the same linguistic root?

Other nocturnal poets are toads and crickets. The toads live in the neighbors' small ornamental pond, and their crooning is pleasant, but the crickets in my own garden cause me sleepless nights and almost drive me out of my mind. "So humble, and hidden, concealed 'mongst the dishes, / Lamenting in crannies, at home in dark fissures"—so Bialik described the cricket in his father's house. But I have looked into this and found that during the day the cricket hides close to the trunks of the same trees it frequents at night. This is how I discovered this "poet of poverty" and relocated it to another part of the moshav, and the problem was solved.

There are other insufferable sounds, first and foremost the barking of dogs left outside by their owners at night. These dogs stand by the dark forest and bark with fear and trembling, hackles raised. Since I live right by the forest, this wakes me up. On the one hand, I am as angry as the next person at being woken up. On the other hand, I am amused at the

absurdity of the whole situation: These dogs are not the wild animals their ancestors were. They are domestic creatures created by man for his own use and pleasure with selective crossbreeding. Food is served to them, and clean water is readily available. They have a roof over their heads and medical insurance. But the real animal kingdom is in the forest, a kingdom of real animals who live real lives, devouring and being devoured in a real forest. Consequently, their nocturnal barking not only expresses fear but a respect for fear.

It really is absurd, but sometimes it dawns on me that my garden is not that different from those dogs. After all, the garden is not really one hundred percent wild. It is true that domesticated dogs are comparable to ornamental plants and, like them, were created by humans, whereas in my garden there are authentic wild plants whose genetics I have not meddled with. But I do help them along by weeding, and I sow them in the right places at the right times. I pamper my garden with extra water when there is a particularly severe heat wave. If I am not mistaken, the garden some-times stands and barks at the forest, realizing that uncompromising nature is over there, a battle for survival is over there, and the real wild, too.

17

A Sorrowful Song

There are two nighttime sounds of which I am particularly fond, and they are lovelier and more thrilling than any other sounds: the song of the stone-curlew choir that I mentioned earlier and will later elaborate on, and the mating call of the scops owl. The stone curlews do not enter the garden but sing in fields near and far, whereas the scops owls occasionally visit me and sing between the branches of my trees, and both, for those of you unfamiliar with them, are types of birds.

In Israel, the scops owl is known as the common hairy, making some people wonder whether this is a species of person living here, but it is a small and sweet owl, the smallest of all owls in Israel. Unlike the stone curlews who sing in unison, perhaps to reinforce and establish relationships within the flock, the scops owl sings a solitary prayer: a song of love and yearning by a lonely male, intended to attract a mate.

This is a hairy serenade, if you please, but much more romantic than any human crooning could ever be. The besotted man sings under the window of his one and only Juliet, whose name and appearance and home he is familiar with, whereas the hairy owl sings to an unfamiliar beloved, nor does he know where she is or if she can hear him. He releases his song into the darkness, hoping it will reach the right ear, and when the lady owl attached to this ear comes to him and consents, they build a family together.

This hairy bird is not a permanent resident of my garden but a migrating bird who arrives in Israel toward spring and remains there until fall. At the end of February or beginning of March, sometimes as late as the beginning of June, I hear him all of a sudden, and I am happy he has come and realize that another year has passed. Unlike the sophisticated love songs of other birds, the scops owl sings a simple song: an exceptionally long series of short, identical cries, persistent and sad, a kind of *kyoot . . . kyoot . . . kyoot* in which the pauses—each about three seconds long—are as precise as the pauses of a metronome. When you see and hear the violent arguments between other males in nature, their flamboyant mating dance, their gleaming colors, their luxuriant tails, their tremendous horns and roars and skirmishes—this small and solitary bird, who expresses his love and yearning and hope with the simplest of calls, arouses affection in the listener and warms the heart.

Since all this happens under cover of night, most humans do not know who is issuing these cries, and there are some who even find the sound objectionable because it is monotonous and interminable. But I know this owl and I know what he is going through and so I have a certain fondness for his cries. Sometimes, when the owl calls from a nearby tree—usually between the jacaranda branches—I even answer him: I try an *ooh . . . ooh . . . ooh* of my own, with the most precise intervals I am able to muster. In this way I try telling the owl that he is not alone in the world and that I am rooting for him. To my great sorrow, the owl does not always understand that my intentions are good. It is quite possible that he is insulted and thinks I am mimicking him in order to ridicule his lack of success with female owls, or perhaps I am a good mimic and he thinks I am another male owl about to steal his mate. Whatever the case, because of these stupid games of mine the owl goes quiet and quickly switches location.

And not just because I mimic him. Like many other creatures, the scops owl is very sensitive to any looks he is given, and even if I do not make a sound but only lift my eyes to the treetop where he hides—he usually sees me, although I cannot see him—there is always a danger he will go silent and fly off to another tree. His flight, like that of all nocturnal raptors, is noiseless, and on a night of a full moon, or by the light of a streetlamp, the owl suddenly appears for a few seconds.

For a moment silence falls over the garden, encompassing the veil of dark, but the scops owl does not fly very far away. He needs to save his strength for his loved one in case she finally deigns to come. He finds a spot close by, and quickly resumes his cries, a pleasant and alluring sound infused with sweetness, designed for the female owl who hides under cover of night, and it is according to the cries of the male owl that she decides if he is hers, and she is his.

I have never seen a female scops owl as she reaches the male, but I am sure this is a wonderfully happy moment. I imagine her, suddenly appearing with her quiet owl's flight, hovering for a moment above the garden and landing on a branch by the male owl.

"Here I am."

Silence. The male owl is beside himself.

"You called so I came."

Silence. The male owl hops abashedly from one leg to another and then fixes two beady eyes on her.

"Don't go," he manages to splutter.

"It's me, my love, why would I go? I'm here."

And all this happens in the garden, right above my head.

18

Anemones

The appearance of the first anemone is a great moment, a moment of revelation. In January, when heavy clouds of lead darken the skies, and a murky aqua-gray adorns the surrounding hills, and winter freeze wraps around the fields, and there are no shimmering flowers or blossoming plants and the heart longs for the beginning of spring—it is then you discover the first anemone."

More's the pity it is not I who wrote these beautiful lines, but my neighbor from Jerusalem, whom I mentioned at the beginning of this book: Amotz Cohen, the naturalist and teacher. The lines appear in *Onot Hashana* (*Seasons of the Year*), published in the 1950s. I recommend that all lovers of nature and the Hebrew language go search for this book in antiquarian bookstores. With a unique style and a learned, poetic manner, Cohen describes nature with all its fauna and flora, from the wasp kingdom to the lichen in the wall, from the snake that sheds its skin to the chaff that flies through the air, the landscape and the soil, the rain clouds and the dry desert wind, traditional Arab agriculture according to the seasons and different tasks with which he became familiar as a child in the village of Motza, where Amotz was the firstborn son.

He goes on to describe the first anemone: "Seemingly, this singular red wonder has somehow found its way here from an unknown world. How did it rise up from the murky ground so delightfully? This firstborn anemone, although a riddle, dignifies the empty field with her majesty."

The anemone is not the first flower to bloom in winter. It is preceded by the cyclamen in my garden. But when the first anemones blossom, the heart fills with happiness, and the garden holds its breath. What else can be said after this beautiful couplet of words written by my teacher and mentor, Amotz Cohen: "red wonder"? It is also of note that the anemone— grand, gleaming, and gushing—does not only stimulate those who see her today, but also stimulated the imagination and creative powers of the ancients, who generated the myth of resurrection.

For the Greeks, the anemone symbolized the drops of blood and wounds of Adonis, a young, handsome fellow who was Aphrodite's lover and was ensnared by the incisors of a wild boar. Aphrodite begged for mercy from Zeus, the champion of Greek gods. He acquiesced and Adonis was resurrected, but only for a single season. Like the anemone, he died at the onset of summer and was resurrected as spring returned.

This lovely story is well known, but in fact its origins are not in Greece but right here. More precisely, it originated with our neighbors, the Phoenicians, who concocted a similar story about a god named Adon. The name "Adon" resembles our own Adonai, Lord, but the two are very different, one from the other. Adonai is a single God, and Adon is one among several. Adonai is an eternal God, one who was not born and does not die, whereas Adon died every year in the heat of summer and was resurrected when winter rains arrived. Since the Phoenicians traveled through the Mediterranean and distributed not only commodities but also ideas and letters and art and stories, their Adon became the Greek Adonis throughout the Western world.

Our forefathers were not concerned with such rituals or idolatry, of course, nor did they compose such stories. But more than once I have wondered why they never took note of the anemone—its color, its freshness, its beauty—to the extent that it is not even mentioned in the Bible. And not just the anemone—very few wildflowers bloom in this book of all books. The Bible includes many plants that relate to working the land, those that are useful to the farmer and those that are harmful—all kinds of fruit trees, wheat, barley, onions, garlic, watermelons, and alongside them thistles and brambles. It also includes aromatic plants, varieties of myrrh, spikenard, and frankincense, which are all related to religious rituals. The thornbush and dill play a starring role in prophecies about destruction, which in the eyes of those who work the land are a symbol of neglect and abandonment; and the vine and fig play a starring role in prophecies about blessings. As for merely lovely flowers—there are almost none.

It seems that even before they went into exile, the Israelites did not feel any particular connection to the wildlife of their country, certainly not anything close to the connection described by the Greeks in their mythological stories, which abound with animals and plants and their deep, complex connections to mankind. The Bible mentions mandrake and turmeric (which appears in the company of spikenard, frankincense, and myrrh and was apparently an aromatic plant rather than the turmeric we know today), the sea lily, and lily of the valley, whose identity is unclear and which various commentators have claimed are daffodils, Madonna lilies, sea pancratium lilies, and various irises. But where are the poppy and the cyclamen, the sea squill, crocus, sternbergia, and buttercup? The hollyhock and the gladiolus and the Agrostemma, chive and chrysanthemum? The lupine and the flax, the Syrian cornflower-thistle and star-of-Bethlehem, the orchid and hyacinth squill? They are all well-known, delightful flowers, neither rare nor hidden from view but conspicuous to the eye, gladdening both God and mankind. All these flowers grew in Israel back then as well, and certainly in greater numbers—and in spite of all this, there is no mention of them in the Bible. Is it possible that no one noticed or admired them, no one felt love for them or happiness when they bloomed and sadness when they wilted? And the lover of the Song of Songs, why did he not weave them into a floral wreath for his beloved? Is it all simply about the work of the land and of God? Is nature only about what is possible and permissible to eat and chop down, and what is not?

Nevertheless, there is a verse in the Bible that might be about anemones. I discovered it in *Words and Their Histories* by the philologist Professor Yechezkel Kutscher, a small book with much to offer, and according to which the anemone is mentioned in the Bible, although not by name. Professor Kutscher recalls a verse from Isaiah in which the prophet describes women who plant *nitei naamanim*, "pleasant plants" that wilt and die in summer, and he attributes this to the rituals of Adon and Adonis and Tamuz—who, along with the women who mourn him, is mentioned in the Bible—all of them young men who died and for whom the ritual of resurrection was generated. Naaman, too, who gave his name to *nitei naamanim*, was a Phoenician god. Professor Kutscher specifies in his book that, to this day, the bloodred anemone is known in Arabic as *shakeyk al-naeman*, "wounds of Naaman." But there is more to it: in Greek the name for this flower is similar to *naaman*, as in English.

"The similarity between *naaman* and anemone is clearly visible," wrote Professor Kutscher, relying both on the Arabic name and the fact that Flavius Josephus tells of the grave belonging to Memnon by the stream close to Belus near Acre, whose name in Hebrew is Naaman and, in Arabic, A-Naamin.

And where does the Hebrew name for anemone, *calanit*, come from? It comes from the Aramaic name for this flower, *calonita*, meaning "small bride." This name perhaps derived from *calil*, "crown" or "wreath," and which also appears under the scientific name of *anemone coronaria*, meaning "crowned anemone."

In short, it is possible that the biblical anemones are indeed those same "pleasant plants." But I still have not found an answer to my question—why do flowers not grow in the Bible?

19

Italy in the Garden

The garden shapes the house and the house shapes the garden. The house overflows into the garden with nooks and corners to nap and sit and work in that are like extra rooms. And the garden penetrates the windows with fragrance and color, shaping life in the kitchen, too. I do not grow vegetables, but I have found wild plants growing in the garden that are edible, and I spice up meals with them. First, chicory can be fried in olive oil and onion as an appetizer. Then there is mallow, similarly prepared, but only when young and fresh. Here and there grows wild garlic, whose leaves I chop and add to salads and omelets. Above all these is the wild asparagus, a pleasing companion to every meal, lean and smaller than its cultured siblings, but superior and more intense in taste, worthy not just as food but as a conversation piece for those who eat it.

I have also brought thyme, white-leaved savory, and sage from the garden, and I enjoy both their aroma and taste. I make a very good pasta sauce with sage. The recipe was given to me by Dr. Eli Landau of blessed memory, a doctor and gastronome, a wise and witty friend, a shoulder to lean on, a keen ear and wide heart. I mourn his absence constantly.

The ingredients: A quantity of good-quality pasta, depending on the number of diners. For this particular dish I recommend pasta that will hold the sauce well, and two diners only, preferably with an air of love between them—and if it is not yet love, then at least affection and curiosity that beg to deepen the relationship.

Butter is also needed, olive oil of the mild variety, dry white wine or semidry, not too sweet and not Chardonnay, a wine which in my opinion is not made from grapes but plywood sawdust. A pinch of salt and, of course, a handful of fresh sage, straight from the garden. If a child is sent to pick the leaves, two handfuls are better, and if the child is very small, then three.

The first rule when making this dish is that it should not be made by both participants in the meal. One person sets to work while the other waits, a glass of chilled white wine in hand, until the dish is ready. In the meantime, the wine sipper can carry on a conversation with the cook, or pester him or her by nuzzling up, depending on how far advanced the relationship is.

The preparation itself is simple. First, divide the handful of sage into two. Tear half the leaves into large pieces, and put aside the others. Heat up a little olive oil in a frying pan and melt the butter, giving it (the exact words written by Dr. Landau in his original recipe) the ripped sage leaves. Sauté briefly on a low flame, add a little water, salt, and white wine. Cover and allow to simmer for a few minutes. Turn off the heat and keep covered with a lid.

Now the rest of the sage leaves are "given" to another pan, sautéed in olive oil at medium heat, and stirred until they are golden brown and crisp, but not blackened or burned, because then they lose their flavor and taste bad. As soon as they are ready, remove them from the frying pan and place on a kitchen towel to soak up excess oil.

Sentence the pasta to death by boiling according to the instructions on the side of the packet, dish the pasta onto the plates, pour the sauce of sage, wine, and butter from the first frying pan onto the pasta. If desired, add a little oil from the second frying pan, stir, sprinkle the browned sage leaves—take care, they easily crumble to the touch—pour more chilled white wine into elegant glasses, and enjoy this dish, which is delicious yet light. Consider this: all the ingredients in this dish indicate good taste. What could be bad about olive oil, wine, and butter? But the real secret to this dish is the addition of crispy sage leaves. These are what lend it character and originality.

The second Italian delicacy is offered by the lemon tree in my garden. I will preface this by saying that despite my love for the fig, blood orange, pomegranate, and pitanga, if I were allowed to plant only one fruit tree, just one, in my garden, I would choose the lemon tree.

The lemon tree is simple and ordinary and does not make any special effort to endear itself to its owners. There are larger and more impressive trees; there are also more reputable and special ones. Its branches are thorny and its fruit sour. Indeed, in contrast to other citrus fruits, nobody peels and eats a lemon the way a clementine or an orange is eaten, and no one squeezes and drinks its juice as though it were grapefruit. The lemon joins only as an addition to a dish or drink, and precisely because of this it is involved, literally, in many meals: I drizzle it onto several dishes, add it to tea or other drinks. And when I use the lemon to season a vegetable salad, I do it the way my mother taught me: I hold half a lemon in the palm of my right hand and squeeze it over a bowl into the palm of my left hand, so the pips remain in my hand and the rest drips through my fingers. After disposing of the pips, I rub my hands together, one wet from the juice and one fragrant from the peel, and it is pleasant for both me and my hands. Not only the fruit of the lemon, by the way, is fragrant, but also its leaves. You can ask for a leaf or two, rub them between your fingers, and enjoy. When the tree blossoms it is worth putting your head between the branches—watch out for thorns!—and swooning.

But aside from these little remembrance ceremonies and the daily use of its nectar, the lemon tree provides me with a remarkable drink: homemade limoncello, the likes of which cannot be compared. I am not bragging. It is very easy to make limoncello, and the quality is determined not by the person making it but by the tree and its fruit. This is why I am willing to offer the recipe to anyone who is interested: the ingredients are 96 percent grain alcohol (watch out for fake bottles!), mineral water, white sugar, and lemons picked from a tree rather than bought in a store. This is critical. Store-bought lemons lose part of their aroma due to the time that elapses after they are picked and also due to an extended period of refrigeration, and their peel is covered in pesticides, wax, and all the other horrors that have only one meaning for the limoncello—rack and ruin.

I wash the dust and dirt from the lemons and carefully peel them, not with a knife but with a good vegetable peeler. That's also important, because it is the outer yellow layer alone that must be peeled. On no account cut through to the white pith under it, because it is bitter. I place these thin yellow peels in large, clean glass jars and then pour the alcohol over them. The ratio is a dozen large lemons to one 750ml bottle of alcohol.

I close the jars hermetically and put them in a dark place, and two to three weeks later, when I take a look at them, I am happy to see that the alcohol has turned yellow. I strain the alcohol and throw the peel into the composter, which makes all the insects and maggots very happy. Otherwise I give them to an aunt or uncle who knows how to bake and who can use the peel to enhance the taste of their cakes. I have been told this by those in the know, although I have neither the knowledge nor the desire to bake cakes and cannot suggest recipes or offer advice.

Now comes the turn of the syrup: I boil mineral water and sugar at the ratio of three parts sugar to five parts water, stir, and make certain that all the sugar has dissolved. I leave it to cool and clarify. The cooling is important, because the syrup is going to be mixed with the alcohol and, if the mixture is hot, some of the alcohol will evaporate as if it never existed.

When mixing the syrup and alcohol, I am scrupulous about the ratio of three parts alcohol to five parts syrup. The reason is not because this is a sanctified ratio but because it is simply to my taste. These ratios can be altered in order to make limoncello that is stronger or weaker, sweeter or sourer. It can be tasted and amended by adding more of one of these ingredients: alcohol, syrup, or water. Fresh, strained lemon juice from the same tree can also be added according to taste. This is the time to note that lemons whose peel is placed in the jars with alcohol should not be thrown away after peeling. Squeeze them and make a lemon concentrate from the juice.

I am in the habit of making two types of limoncello, 40 percent and 25 percent, and to serve it according to the time of day, the company, and the circumstances. By the way, the tasting stage, amendments, and return tastings are extremely nice and rich in possibilities, particularly if you cannot decide right away, and then you taste again, and again. For this reason, I advise leaving the tasting stage until after work, not before driving, and in the company of the same person with whom you ate the sage pasta.

I recommend drinking the limoncello ice cold. I store the bottles of 40 percent in the freezer without worrying that they will freeze over, and I keep the bottles of 25 percent in the refrigerator and place one in the freezer about an hour before serving. And another important point: there are friends who, after a single swig of the limoncello, ask me to gift them a bottle, and after three swigs they no longer ask but demand loudly that I do so. It must be made clear that this is simply not possible, because the rumor that the world's best bottles of limoncello are given out here spreads like wildfire, and people begin appearing, asking, begging, and even threatening. I must set the record straight at this early stage in order to dispel the slightest grain of hope on this matter.

Everything written here in this chapter is intended to say one thing, that it is good for a person to have a lemon tree in his garden. If you don't have a garden, a lemon tree can be planted at the entrance to your apartment block. If the neighbor who opposes everything opposes this, too, a lemon tree can be grown in a large pot on the balcony. The lemon tree is hardier and stronger than other citruses and grows nicely in mountainous regions, too, but in areas like that the lemon tree can be helped if planted by a stone wall that faces south, so that at night the heat of the sun stored up during the day will be emitted in the direction of the lemon tree.

And one more thing: if you are emigrating from Israel, you should plant a lemon tree in your new location in order to preserve something of your own identity. But remember that the lemon tree may feel distress in cold places like Berlin or Montreal, so I recommend emigrating to Sicily, California, Australia, Greece, and other places where lemons will also be happy. Plant a lemon tree in your new front yard, and when you get homesick, inhale the scent of a leaf, fruit, or flower, and you will feel better right away.

20

Grass

I have already noted the bedraggled, neglected lawn that was here when I first arrived. At first, with the power of an involuntary reflex, I revived the lawn. I gave it water, fertilizers, and I mowed it for a number of years. Finally, I had second thoughts and got rid of it. This is how I let both the garden and myself know that from that time forth I would grow only wild-flowers. But it was a much deeper declaration—that I was integrating into the surrounding areas. There would be no more distinguished strangers from Wimbledon and South Africa, only local plants.

Now is the time to clarify that my spatial integration is botanic in principle. Although I live in the Middle East, I am bound to it with ropes of emotion, culture, and rooted history. I have no interest in becoming part of regional norms and practices, such as mixing religion and politics, the business of revenge and honor, discrimination and violence against women, overzealous respect for tradition and a fundamental revulsion for democracy. A person can decide for himself within which den of inequity he chooses to rest his aching head. Aside from that, there are plenty of people around me who fit into this area far better than I do, and consequently I dare say that integration will get by just fine without me.

What is the connection between this and getting rid of grass in my garden? The grass we know, the type that grows on soccer pitches, in public parks, in well-manicured private gardens, and on kibbutzim, is not a local wild plant but an imported conception of European gardening. I am aware that "grass" is the first botanic name to be mentioned in the Bible, in the very first chapter, and I also remember from this same chapter that the land brought forth what is literally translated as "grass of weed" even before the first trees were grown. But the grass of biblical Hebrew is not a particular plant but a mixture of local wild weeds, sprouting in winter and providing sustenance to herds of cows and goats and wild animals, and these weeds yellow and wither at the end of spring, whereas the European lawn is a foreign implant—precisely that—in our region of the world. It is planted and sowed and fertilized and mowed, and most important, in contrast to the natural biblical grass that is at the mercy of heaven, it must be copiously watered throughout the summer, because it was raised that way back home and because the owners of the lawn want it to be evergreen.

In Israel the lawns of Labor-affiliated communities are famous, especially those of the kibbutzim. Not all of them, only those still able to afford the cost of irrigation. More than any other component of Hebrew gardening, the lawns were established in defiance of the local climate and as a defense shield from it. This is not intended as criticism. The kibbutz founders—today we tend to forget, obliterating the immensity of this enterprise and the obstacles they overcame—lived for years in tents and shacks, on harsh terrain that was scorching, exposed, dusty, muddy, and thorny. Aside from rendering and cultivating this into arable land, they also sowed and planted ornamental trees and bushes inside the kibbutz, because they recognized the need for shade and coolness and a sense of home and civilization. At first they planted large quick-growing trees.

Later, they sowed expansive lawns that covered numerous public areas of the kibbutz. A lawn cools the air, reduces the amount of dust, provides a place in which to sit or stretch out, alone or in the company of others. A lawn is pleasing to the eye, it widens the mind and the gaze. Due to its green color, it infuses an atmosphere of order and cleanliness, of life and blossoming.

The lawn by the dining room of the kibbutz is usually called the big lawn. It is a quintessential characteristic of the kibbutz landscape. It is the softer and pleasanter side of the Zionist promise to dress the Land of Israel "in a frock of cement and mortar," and is one of the flagships of an equal society—the grass belongs to everybody—and of coping with heat waves, mud, and dust and facing the caprices of fate and nature.

From a certain point of view, the large kibbutz lawn is reminiscent of the sidewalks paved over sand dunes in the early days of Tel Aviv. In *A Small Town and People Few,* Nahum Gutman describes those returning from the nearby Arab Jaffa, stomping on these sidewalks to rid their clothes and shoes of mire and dust.

"The stomping they stomped declared this: We want a paved town. Straight streets. Gardens. Parks. Security. Civilization. We do not want the vicissitudes of fate, nor do we want trachoma. Or veiled faces. We do not want *A Thousand and One Arabian Nights.* This stomping was a program for life, a political declaration." Or in other words: We will not integrate! We will pave and build and plant Europe right here.

The years went by. The founders' sons and their grandchildren, born and raised in this country and under its sun, became acquainted with and learned to love its nature and were not alarmed by the scorching, the prickly, the stinging, and the barren that had terrified their forefathers. Evidence of this are the beloved and knowledgeable descriptions of landscape and nature of S. Yizhar, and I also remember lines from a poem called "Thorn" written by my father, Yitzhak Shalev, on a trail he hiked in Europe. He referred to it as "the grassy, smooth Europe" and also "the land of rejoicing grass," and then continued to a description of his yearning for local thorns, the Middle Eastern ones, "the thorn of impoverished Canaan," with these words: "To it I yearn in those meadows of green—"

> *It is the thorn that wrestled with dying and alive remained,*
> *While every grass in the field withered away and every wild*
> *green shriveled.*

I do not grow thorns in my garden, but neither do I grow grass, and the summer days when "the hay withers away and the grass faileth," when my garden wilts, dries up, and becomes ugly, do not alarm me. On the contrary, this is how we integrate. We integrate into a larger and more ancient area than the present Middle East. I like to see how, within my modest garden, great stories of death and resurrection are realized, stories of other nations who lived here—the Phoenicians, the Sumerians, the Egyptians, and the Greeks—stories sourced in the changing of seasons, the withering and sprouting of plants, in creative imagination and love and familiarity with nature of the ancient people, becoming one of the founding stones of human civilization.

I write these lines at the beginning of summer. My garden is already dry, and the grass in the neighbor's garden is greener than the grass I do not have. But the hollyhocks and the splendid bindweed and the Agrostemma fleck it with purple and pink, and dozens of sea squills will soon shoot up from the hard earth to air that is no less hard, and after that the preschool children will come visit the squills, as they do every year. They will sit around the squills and sing them songs of celebration and autumn. Later, it will rain and the garden will blossom and turn green, returning to life until next summer.

A Prayer for Rain

Every squirrel, ant, and bee knows that the larder must be stocked before winter comes. And it is not just these creatures who cope with the intrinsic difficulties of nature but also their literary brethren. I have already mentioned the love for home felt by the protagonists of *The Wind in the Willows,* and now I will add a description of a visit by Rat and Mole to the home of their friend and protector, Mr. Badger: a snowstorm rages outside but in the large kitchen a fire burns in the hearth, and stored in the larders are baskets of eggs and ham and dried herbs and piles of apples, turnips, potatoes, baskets full of nuts, and jars of honey.

A winter storeroom is also described in Willa Cather's *My Ántonia,* whose plot takes place in frozen Nebraska at the beginning of the twentieth century: the cellar of a farming family in which there are summer fruits and casks of all kinds of preserves and pickles. *My Ántonia,* by the way, is a wonderful novel, and I recommend it to anyone looking for a good book to read.

And above all, here is the end of Bialik's "Summer Is Dying":

Soon a day of cloud and rain
Taps softly on the windowpane.
Did you mend your shoes!
Patch your mantle for this day?
Go forth, stock up on potatoes.

These words are beautifully poetic and cause the heart to sigh, but where I live the English winter of Kenneth Grahame does not exist, nor the Ukrainian winter of Bialik or the North American winter of Willa Cather. Apart from a few sociable insects, and perhaps a mole rat in hidden cellars, no one hoards food here in anticipation of winter. Our existential worries are directed at our reservoirs of water, namely the Sea of Galilee, and we hear endless reports and forecasts on its famous water levels, like certain people who are never satisfied and can never get enough. What height is it? Is it going up or down? Has enough water accumulated in the Sea of Galilee? Can I water my citrus trees this summer?

I remember thinking this when I read *The Gardener's Year* by the Czech writer Karel Capek. In it, Capek describes his work in his ornamental garden month after month, for an entire year. I felt envy while reading—this time not writer's envy but gardener's—because Capek hardly refers to the subject of water and irrigation. There is a nice description of watering with a hose, but there is no mention of conserving water, because in the Czech Republic there is precipitation of all sorts throughout the year, and in the Middle East we harbor a traditional and constant anxiety that there will be a drought, even in the modern era of drip irrigation systems, purification plants, and desalination facilities. Not all of us, to my great shame and sorrow, because it is always possible to see some delinquent washing his car or hosing down his yard and to be annoyed at the waste of good water as it flows to the ground, but usually the citizens of Israel are mindful of the scarcity of water, and even the secular types among us pray for rain.

Regrettably, the official prayer for rain does not always work. This fact is well known, and the reason for it is twofold. First, our religious leaders are not good enough, and God no longer talks and listens to them the way he used to. Second, the writers of our rain prayers are not farmers but rabbis, and there are considerations involved that are off topic and might even sound strange. To begin with, look at the timing of this prayer: it is said on the last day of Sukkoth, the Feast of the Tabernacles, because the branches that cover the traditional sukkah do not really form roofs and the Jewish people want to sit in their sukkahs without worrying about getting wet in the rain. In other words, the mitzvah of sitting in the sukkah takes precedence over the needs of nature and agriculture. It is enough that God understands that those praying to Him for rain are not serious people, that they are more worried about their own personal comfort rather than the real needs of the world and the different creatures within it.

The actual content of the prayer for rain is also problematic. It is an unprofessional brief that does not define well the needs of its clients. This means it does not clarify to God exactly which rain to bring down, where and when and how much. This phenomenon is particularly evident in the story of the most celebrated rain man, Honi the Circle Drawer.

At the beginning of the story a severe drought is depicted: "Once it happened that the greater part of the month of Adar [winter's end] had gone and yet no rain had fallen. The people sent a message to Honi the Circle Drawer, Pray that rain may fall."

Honi had quite a reputation in that sphere, and indeed displayed self-confidence in his powers. He even responded to those who approached him with a boastful answer: "Go and bring in the Pesach ovens, so that they will not dissolve in the rain." Pesach ovens were made of clay and perhaps mud, placed in the yards for use at Pesach. The holiday was approaching, and Honi, sure of his success, warned those who approached him that the rain he was about to bring down might damage their ovens.

He prayed and no rain fell. What did he do? He thereupon drew a circle in the ground and stood within it and exclaimed before God: Master of the Universe! Your children have turned to me because they see that I am as a member of your household. I swear by your great name, that I will not move from here until you have mercy upon your children. Rain began to drip (weak rain fell, not more than a drizzle).

And his disciples said to him: We believe that this rain came down merely to release you from your oath. Thereupon he exclaimed: It is not for this that I have prayed, but for rain to fill cisterns, ditches and caves (heavy rains that will fill all sorts of reservoirs).

The rain then began to come down with great force. Every drop being as big as the opening of a barrel. His disciples then said to him: Master, we believe that the rain came down to destroy the world. Thereupon he exclaimed before [God]. It is not for this that I have prayed, but for rain of benevolence, blessing and bounty. Then rain fell normally until the Israelites in Jerusalem were compelled to go up [for shelter to the Temple Mount] because of the rain [that did not stop and flooded the lower areas].

[His disciples then said to him] Master, in the same way as you have prayed for the rain to fall, pray for the rain to cease.

And Honi prayed again, and "immediately the wind began to blow and the clouds were dispersed and the sun shone." There is certainly arrogance in Honi the Circle Drawer's behavior, and also something childish and self-indulgent. It is somewhat strange to see God, a usually serious and purposeful character who is not always the fountain of patience, cooperating with this behavior. But the important point is that the prayer makes clear to God precisely what is wanted by the supplicants. In the case of a prayer for rain, do not request "mercy upon thy children," a too-general formulation, and do not pray for rain "to fill cisterns, ditches and caves," which indicates lack of thought and carelessness concerning possible consequences, nor should one pray for "rain of benevolence, blessing and bounty," which turns into rain of fury and destruction when the beginning and end are not specified. You must specify the kind of rain you want, its duration and location, in a manner that God can understand.

Although my connections to God are not as good as Honi's, I sometimes pray for rain as well. I admit that the wording of my prayers is not designed for the needs of the public at large or according to principles of faith. They are worded according to my own needs and those of my garden, but they are very clear and precise. And so, although better Jews than I sit in their sukkahs, I ask for a few hefty portions of rain before the Sukkoth holiday and also on the holiday itself, to persuade the wild grass to sprout before I sow my flowers. And then I add another request, that after the rain there will be a week of sunshine in which I can till them, uproot and exterminate them. And then I ask for another decent amount of rain, so that I can sow my seeds in well-watered soil, an expression that God is familiar with, understands, and remembers from the Bible.

From this time onward I ask for blessed rain devoid of long intervals, so that my flowers will neither blossom too early nor bloom all at once, and in the spring I ask for two more lots of rain: one around Pesach and the other two to three weeks after that so that flowering will continue,

giving new seeds the possibility of developing in comfort and suitably swelling up before finally ripening.

I know my prayers for rain are selfish and rather annoying, but on the other hand—is there anything God cannot do? Worshippers with more difficult and egocentric requests have come and gone. Aside from that, it's a fact that there are years in which God responds favorably to my prayers, and if He dawdles, I do not hesitate in turning to Zeus and Baal, because I am in favor of competition. When my prayers are answered, it is not only my garden and I who benefit, but other gardens and gardeners, and the forest and the field, their creatures and plants, and the entire natural world—and if, here and there, Jews get soaked while sitting in their sukkahs, it is no great calamity. The Jewish people have survived much worse.

22

Chopping Down

When I came to this house, a large chinaberry stood in the garden. Even though this is not a native tree but an ornamental, imported one—I loved it, the smell of its blossoms, its crown that resembles a canopy, and its height of thirty feet. I loved watching the nesting of the woodpeckers in the holes they had pecked there, but at the time it did not occur to me that these amiable woodpeckers would decide the chinaberry's fate.

The woodpecker also nests in the pecan and eucalyptus, but when it sees a chinaberry tree it will always favor that for its soft core. It perforates the tree's bark with its formidable beak, penetrating inside, widening and creating a space for use as a room for the goslings, and builds a nest there. These internal spaces weaken the tree, which is not strong at the best of times. And indeed, several years after my arrival here, a large branch broke close to where the trunk splits, falling and thumping to the ground three feet from where I was working in the garden. At the point of breakage, the branch was hollow, and I could see the remains of a nest.

My common sense told me to cut down the tree, but I took pity on it. Less than two weeks later, another branch fell. When it comes to a chinaberry, no official permission is needed to chop it down. In the past it was a common and beloved tree, but today it is regarded as an invasive species and a dangerous tree. I summoned my young friend Gal, a woodcutter and pruner of trees. He showed up with a tractor that had a folding hydraulic arm, the kind used to repair traffic lights and hang flags. He stood on a platform at the end of the arm, equipped with a short electric saw he held in one hand, and began to circle the chinaberry. He first removed the treetop's thin branches and then proceeded to work on the thicker ones, until nothing remained but the skeleton of the trunk and a few large limbs, devoid of foliage. Once its boughs were removed, the tree also lost its color. The green torso, pulsating with life, became a black silhouette against a gray firmament, a skeleton with hands outstretched, a monument on the back of a gravestone. My friend Gal hovered around it dejectedly, the saw rattling in his hand, felling one section after another.

The chopping down of a tree is a difficult sight, but actually a carefully planned one is even harder on the eye and the heart. In a residential neighborhood it is impossible to cut down a large tree from the base of the trunk because it might fall with all its weight onto a roof, a person, car, or other plants in a garden. This is why Gal cut it down limb by limb, a slow execution. But because of his professionalism and experience, his movements did not manifest themselves as the violent touch of death but as gestures of attention, and even love.

In Pirkei D'Rabbi Eliezer it is written: "When a tree that bears fruit is cut down, its moan goes from one end of the world to the other, yet no sound is heard." This is beautifully worded and has a certain Zen quality to it, arousing envy for its very elegance, but the content is disappointing because it has a utilitarian, anthropocentric attitude that is in fact expressed in the term "a tree that bears fruit": all trees bear fruit, since it is the fruit that contains the seeds, but man bestows the honorable title of "fruit tree" only on those trees bearing fruit deemed edible. All the other trees are described insultingly as "barren trees." The word "barren" suggests emptiness—a continuation of the perception outlined in Genesis that nature and all its creatures were created for the benefit and enjoyment of that pinnacle of creation, mankind.

Whether or not they produce fruit we can eat and enjoy, trees possess qualities common to humans and animals: they are born and die; they eat, drink, multiply, grow, fall sick; they sense light, heat, touch, moisture, and perhaps even time. Some of them actually have the ability to move— toward the sun, for example, or in search of support or something to cling to. One of my olive trees, for example, does not like the big terebinth tree that grows beside it and clearly inclines away, distancing its branches from those of the terebinth.

Do trees feel pain? I doubt it. Do they shout out in their suffering? Despite what is written in Pirkei D'Rabbi Eliezer, I further doubt this. I do, however, agree that if they feel pain and cry out, humans cannot hear their voices, since they are not able to hear and understand anything that so differs from them.

At this stage, Gal lowered the arm of the crane, sliced the thick bifurcated branches, and cut the trunk into circular slices. The pieces fell with heavy thuds to the ground. The sounds as they hit the ground, from a steadily decreasing height, gradually changed, from the mighty thump of the first one to the soft, dull blow of the final one, the last one. Gal climbed off the crane, sliced the last few sections of what was once a trunk, silenced the saw, and put it aside.

We sat down to drink a glass of cold water. "There goes my good mood," he said. "I hate chopping trees down to the ground. I'd rather prune it and save it, but there was no choice here."

The boughs—spindly branches that bore leaves—he piled onto his cart to throw away on the dumping ground. He would use the chunks of thick branches and trunk for heating. In the picture that is framed by my kitchen window there is an empty space, like a mouth after a tooth is extracted, and in my heart—only sorrow and unease.

23

Poppies

The poppy is a flower I like a lot, and I gather and sow its seeds in the garden every year. But before I talk about it I would like to stress to the readers, particularly those who are policemen or judges—that the poppy growing in my garden is not cultured but wild. It is not the *Papaver somniferum,* whose growth is a felony.

The meaning of this Latin name is "opium poppy" or "dream carrier." It is known by this name because it contains anesthetics, and from the fluid stored in the lining of its capsules opium is produced and distilled into heroin. Incidentally, the seeds within the capsules are also used to make drugs that are no less addictive—poppy seed cake. Any reader unfamiliar with addiction to poppy seed cake will not understand what I am talking about. But those in the know will nod their heads in love and yearning, and perhaps wistfulness, because all these addicts harbor memories of a longed-for poppy seed cake. Sometimes they come across something similar, but it is never the thing itself, and the rest is history.

In short, the poppies I grow in my garden are the ones that bloom in the spring in various places around Israel, and I dare say they are known to many. It is true that the blossoming of the anemones is better promoted, enjoys aggressive public relations, and garners more attention, but to my mind the poppy fields are more beautiful. I know of several, and I visit them every spring.

The poppy is the last of the "great red" quartet that adorns our countryside from the middle of winter through the end of spring, and it flowers after the anemone, tulip, and Asian buttercup. In color, size, and cyclic blossoming and withering these flowers have become a symbol of and a shrine to young men whose blood has been spilled, from the aforementioned heroes of ancient mythology to the casualties of contemporary war.

The poet Haim Gouri wrote about the fallen soldiers of the Lamed-Heh convoy in "Here Lie Our Bodies": "We will meet again," he writes, "returning as red flowers," and in "Bab el Wad" he writes:

> A spring day will come and cyclamens bloom
> Anemones redden the hilltop and slope.
> You who will walk here, on the path that we trod
> Never forget us—we are Bab el Wad.

My father, the poet Yitzhak Shalev, wrote a poem about the fallen soldiers at Sha'ar Hagai. The name of the poem is "Gray Rusting Skeletons," and it includes this line: "Oh you, blood reddening the ribs of your chests like poppies." And the poet Natan Yonatan wrote in "There Are Flowers":

> Did you see such rubies
> Shouting far and wide,
> Once a field of blood
> Now a field of poppies.

In England and its former colonies, the poppy is worn in memory of the fallen, all because of a poem that was written in World War I. As in Natan Yonatan's poem, the poppies are described as blooming in the battlefields and military graveyards. The poem, "In Flanders Fields," was written by John McCrae, a Canadian military physician, in memory of his comrades who fell during that war:

> *In Flanders fields the poppies blow*
> *Between the crosses, row on row,*
>   *That mark our place; and in the sky*
>   *The larks, still bravely singing, fly*
> *Scarce heard amid the guns below.*
>
> *We are the Dead. Short days ago*
> *We lived, felt dawn, saw sunset glow,*
>   *Loved and were loved, and now we lie,*
>   *In Flanders fields.*

There are various types of wild poppies in Israel, which laymen like me have difficulty differentiating among, and so we call them all poppies, but the erudite and the purists know them and can distinguish among them, and they demand that poppies from the south should not be planted in the north and vice versa, because they pollinate each other and produce undesirable hybrids.

There is more: in the life of a poppy there are a few more interesting phenomena that I was unaware of, although they happen in my garden, right under my nose. It was Professor Avi Shmida, the botanist, who revealed them to me.

It happened when we went out to a poppy field symbolically close to Kibbutz Netiv HaLamed-Heh, named after the thirty-five members of a convoy who fell in battle in 1948. Professor Shmida listened patiently to my poeticisms on how poppies move in the breeze, and how in Monet's *Poppy Field* you can feel that breeze, and then he turned my attention to a few poppies that were virtually dancing, even when the breeze died down. He pulled the petals of one poppy apart with his fingers to show me a beetle crawling along and wallowing inside the poppy energetically, causing the flower to palpably move and tremble.

It has been explained to me that the poppy, and the other great reds, too, lack nectaries. These beetles visit the flowers to eat pollen and take advantage of this wonderful opportunity to discover they can also meet a mate there for an hour of pleasuring. In other words, the flowers of the anemone, the tulip, the Asian buttercup, and the poppy are not just restaurants but hotel rooms that specialize in that kind of thing.

This information immediately turned me from an amateur botanist to a voyeur zoologist. I snatched my eyeglasses off my face, pushed my nose up against the poppy flower, and observed from close up what was happening within. This is the advantage of nearsighted people whose eyes turn to magnifying glasses after the age of fifty. Indeed, I saw two ladybirds, one carrying its mate on its back—and by the look on their faces, they were not practicing piggybacks but something else altogether.

I asked: Why does the anemone bloom in the middle of winter, a difficult season, and not in the spring, like the poppy? Professor Shmida explained that there is a temporal gap between the great red flowers: the anemone blooms first, then the tulips, after that the Asian buttercup, and, finally, the poppy. All this is to ensure the beetles won't bring anemone pollen to the Asian buttercup or poppy pollen to the tulip—a waste of pollen that will grow nothing.

On this particular hike, I also learned that the color red has a further advantage: it is a signpost, warning cattle not to eat them. Indeed, not only the cultivated poppy but also the wild one and other red flowers contain

substances that are unhealthy. Cows and sheep learn to avoid them, and this is why anemones and poppies are prevalent in pastureland.

It is not, however, just the cattle, but also the beetles who know of these toxins, and they use it shrewdly. Professor Shmida turned my attention to the fact that the majority of poppy flowers are scratched and bruised. He explained that the beetles scratch the surface and then eat the toxins secreted by the flower. In this way, they themselves become toxic, and birds learn not to eat them—evolution is indeed one of the wisest things created by God.

I returned home and immediately went out to examine my own garden. I discovered the poppies to be crawling with beetles. Indeed, the poppy petals were scratched, and I was sorry I had not noticed this myself. Then I remembered further lines written by my father, and I was ashamed I had not thought of them while in the company of Professor Shmida, lines from "Light on the Waters of Ginosar" depicting a coast-to-coast hike, from the shores of the Mediterranean to the shores of the Sea of Galilee. My father describes the nature scene thus:

A youth picks a flower and catches a beetle in his hand,
Twitching, drowning in scarlet silk . . . the colors love each
  other.
The poppies expand their chests, revealing black hearts
To tender flax maidens, who modestly hide their growth.

This poem surprised me with its astute observation and knowledge because my father, an avid hiker who knew Israel well, mostly focused on the Bible and history when hiking and was less concerned with flora and fauna. I even remember the day my mother persuaded him to join her on a hike with the Society for the Protection of Nature, and he returned highly amused.

"How was it?" I asked.

"We set out," he said, "and after six hundred feet we saw a grasshopper and we protected it. We continued on for another half a mile, saw a bulbul and protected that, too. Later we saw a sea squill, protected that one as well, and then we came home."

I always knew my father was more knowledgeable than I about the Bible, Hebrew, literature, and history, and I consoled myself with the fact that I knew more about nature. But now I discovered that even here my father had a sharper eye than I. It's a fact: he noticed the beetle within the poppy flower, although he never showed a particular interest in either beetles or poppies, and he did this on his own, without the expert advice of botany professors.

24

Moments of Bliss

The wild garden bestows not only interest, knowledge, pleasure, and satisfaction—but also moments of bliss upon its owner. Most of these moments are seasonal and predictable, but this does not decrease the happiness and delight they bring. These are the moments of budding and blooming, the return of winter or summer birds, moments of that same breeze I described, blowing through the section of the garden where poppies bloom, and also the emergence of the sea squill's green leaves after it has flowered and wilted. It is the same for the sprouting of the lupines I sow, the moment their first leaflets emerge and rise up, looking like tiny hands, beseeching heaven from the earth below. And also the sprouting of cyclamen seeds because, in contrast to the first leaflets of many other flowers that differ greatly from the leaves of the mature plant, the first leaf of a cyclamen looks exactly like that of a mature one, aside from its size—it is very small—and aside from the design unique to each cyclamen which appears on every single one of its leaves after the first year.

There are also moments of bliss generated by animals and insects. Like the song of bees that resonates from within the oak and the buckthorn, surprising and delighting me anew, because the flowers of these trees are not as prominent and alluring as, for example, the flowers of the Judas tree or styrax. They are minuscule, without color or fragrance, but the bees come to them for free meals of pollen. By January's end, when a warm sunny day suddenly lights up, it is possible to hear them within the tree, as if a contrabass and cello are playing there. Their hum is deep and soft, but distinctly audible as it rises up, filling the air.

When I heard this magnificent choir for the first time I did not understand what I was listening to until I drew close to the oak, lifted my head, and discovered that the sound was emerging from within the branches. Hundreds of bees were toiling away there, gathering pollen from the flowers and buzzing wildly. I went under the tree's canopy, stood by the trunk, closed my eyes, and sank down into the bee's song from head to toe, and since then I do it every year. What a magnificent concert this is, refined and deep, warm and intense, signifying that bees do not perceive springtime as we do: Our own springtime is colorful and fragrant and warm and arousing and caressing, pleasant to the eye, the skin, and the nose, pulling at the heart and then the body—to go out, to hike, to inhale, see, love. The bees, however, come out in springtime in order to work. They do not talk about "cyclamen hills" and do not tell of "carpets of anemones." Their springtime has a purely economic meaning: the hive is full of hungry mouths, the larder is bare during the rainy winter, flower pollen and nectar must be brought to produce honey, feed the queen and the larvae, and raise another generation of workers. I enjoy listening to their song, but enjoy even more knowing that I am not one of them—bees, ants, and other societies in which bondage is inherited, a tradition so sanctified that it can never be changed.

A further moment of bliss for me is when a hedgehog or tortoise appears in the garden. I love hedgehogs and tortoises, and every year I see fewer and fewer of them. But occasionally they appear, filling my heart with joy. Once, at dusk, as I sat on the ground in the garden, a female hedgehog came with her two small hoglets, whose spines had not quite stiffened. They went hither and thither with the deportment of wheelers

and dealers; they searched, they sniffed, and they passed close by, so close that one of the hoglets brushed up against me. Such proximity to a wild animal, even a mere hedgehog, is one of trust and confidence, and this brings great pleasure.

And birds, too. In the surrounding area, as well as in my garden, are hoopoes, ravens, turtledoves, sunbirds, laughing doves, parakeets, snake eagles, bulbuls, blackbirds, warblers, tufted titmice, robins and white-breasts, Syrian woodpeckers, barn owls, scops owls, stone curlews, partridges, larks, falcons, jaybirds, and sparrows. I recognize them by appearance and also voice. Just before dawn, when I awaken, I can tell the time according to which bird is singing outside.

I've heard the calls of all these birds, except for that of the snake eagle. The blackbird and the bulbul are the pleasantest singers, but I also love hearing the white-breasted kingfisher, a bird that no longer plucks its food out of the water but dives down to the ground, ensnaring lizards and insects. In the morning it releases loud laughter above my garden, announcing to me that it is his alone. But the garden also belongs to the sunbird who, despite its tiny proportions, also declares ownership in a sharp, courageous voice, and the parakeet, too, an invasive bird who behaves like the lord of the manor. They banish woodpeckers from my garden, not because God has promised them this plot of land, but because they crave the nesting cavities that have been dug into the tree trunks. The garden also belongs to the robin, returning to me from Europe each year, reminding me and all the other birds that the garden is not mine, nor theirs, but the robin's.

This is my second robin. The first one arrived in my second or third winter here, perching on the terebinth tree near the window, rendering war cries and shrill, aggressive tut-tutting. "*Tut! Tut! Tut!* Take off!" I have seen it more than once guarding its borders, and the spectacle is an amusing one: a small, tubby bird hopping valiantly from branch to branch: "*Tut! Tut! Tut!* All trespassers will die!"

At the beginning of summer, the robin returned to its homeland, and the following winter, when the *Tut! Tut! Tut!* and its robin came back, I asked someone who told me that in all likelihood it is the very same robin, coming back to its winter residence. But small songbirds do not live long, and I was deeply sorry the winter this robin failed to reappear on the terebinth tree, a few years after it first arrived.

For some years I lived without robins, until the gods sent me a new one. One cold and wintry morning, I heard it and rushed outside, overwhelmed with happiness. It had arrived: tut-tutting energetically, guarding its estate from strangers and invaders. In spite of its socialist colors and thin, straight beak, the robin is extremely hawkish.

The sunbird has also given me a moment of great bliss or, more precisely, a moment of pain and regret that turned into joy. The sunbird, also known by its old Hebrew nickname that translates as "honey-sucker," is the smallest bird in my garden. Sometimes—very rarely—a warbler appears, competing for this title, but the sunbird is almost always around. The females are brown-gray, and the iridescent males shimmer green and black with every movement of their bodies.

More than once I have seen them hovering above the flowers like tiny helicopters, and the sight is really lovely, except that under this miniature sweetness hides a hot-tempered, aggressive, and impetuous creature. The males chase one another above the garden and between the branches, and they fight their own reflections, mirrored in windowpanes. They rise and fall and change direction with a dexterity that would make fighter planes and their pilots jealous, and they fear nothing, neither other sunbirds nor any other type of bird, nor animals or humans. When I see them, I recall a lovely description by Nahum Gutman that appeared in *In the Land of Lobengulu King of Zulu*. It describes a voyage in South Africa, and how a honey-sucker—Gutman uses the old name for the sunbird—intimidated a baboon who came too close to its nest: "When the monkey drew nearer toward the location of the nest, the honey-sucker began disturbing the world. The tweets frequently exited her throat one after the other, like gunshots. She jumped toward the monkey, gyrated around him, flew upon him . . . This is what happens when there are two eggs in the nest. Size is not important."

Once I damaged a sunbirds' nest in my garden, and I regret it to this day. I was pruning the lavender bushes that grow on one of the garden terraces, and I noticed how the entire time two sunbirds hovered above me, a male and a female, calling loudly. At the time, I did not understand they were trying to banish me from the vicinity. I thought they were occupied with the usual business of sunbirds, an argument between neighbors, or courtship and betrayal. It was only when the pruning shears struck their nest, suspended and concealed within the thicket, that I finally understood. By then it was too late. The nest disconnected and collapsed; the two minuscule eggs contained within it fell and shattered. The sunbirds departed and did not return to the garden that summer, and I was afraid they would never come back. But the next summer they returned once again—either the same sunbirds or another pair—and I rejoiced with great joy and since then have kept my eyes open and taken better care.

The birds that bestow the greatest bliss on me do not live in my garden but in the adjacent field. These are the stone curlews—fowl that can fly but prefer to walk and run. They are the size of pullets, their legs are long, their eyes yellow, and their gaze a fierce one. Their feathers are fashioned into a camouflaged costume of yellows and browns and grays. When the stone curlews stand motionless, the eye cannot see them, but at night their calls can be heard from afar. Shortly after sunset, and in the middle of the night and at predawn, they hold folk-dance festivals and sing-alongs that are popular here in the valley. There is something mysterious and attractive about these gatherings that appeals to me. On summer nights, when the stone curlews sing and dance in the reaped field below my house, I sometimes go down there, edging toward them in the darkness. I am careful not to get too close, because then they fall silent and flee. I stop at a distance of a hundred feet from them and lie supinely on the ground, gazing up at the sky and listening.

Lying on the ground under vast and deep summer skies, listening to the stone curlews' strange and mysterious voices, endows this moment with an air of dreaming with open eyes. Regrettably, I see neither ladders nor angels, but a person must make do with what he or she has. And at this moment I am blessed with a warm night and soft soil, devoid of stones, and skies filled with stars, and stone curlews singing me a song—and this is so much more than most people have, and so much more than I have at many other moments.

25

Land

In Hebrew, the word for land and earth and soil is *adama,* a word that is closely rooted to *adom* (red) and *dam* (blood), but most important is the word "Adam"—son of the earth, named after the earth from which he was created and to which he will return. *Adama* is the mother of every plant and animal and has also given birth to a few highly charged Hebrew expressions—the land of our fathers, working the land, virgin land, holy land, motherland—but I am talking about land in its simplest meaning, the soil on the ground, the material we stand on which is sowed and planted and within which my plants root themselves, the very substrate on which my bare feet tread.

There are several types of soil in Israel. Those in the know use words like "rendzina," "alluvial," "peat," and "terra rossa" the same way I use "diacritical mark," "low range," and "over easy." But even laymen like myself can distinguish between the heavy dark soil of the valley and the light pale soil of the coast, between the red loam of the Sharon area and the white marlstone of the southern Dead Sea and northern Arava. The truth is that you do not have to go from one end of the country to another. Even within the limited boundaries of my garden the soil changes from place to place, from one corner to another.

As I have already explained, my garden extends across a slope. The soil is rich and dense in the lower section, but porous and light higher up. Here it is brown and there it is blackened, here it is reddish, and there it is permeable and drains easily, and here puddles form, and here it smells like this and there it smells like that. All this is because my house straddles the border between the Jezreel Valley and the Lower Galilee. It is precisely on the border: the short slope upon which it is built is part of the first hills of the Galilee, and the lower part of the garden composes one of the perimeters of the valley. Each side has its own temperature—early morning it is easy to sense that the lower section of the garden is colder than the upper section, and each side has its own soil and plants. The cyclamens, for example, prefer the upper side; the daffodils prefer the lower; the sea squill is happy in both places.

And there is other soil in the garden or, more precisely, soil that was brought here: a few cubic feet of special soil, with extraordinary growing properties. Perhaps the vestiges of soil from the Garden of Eden, and perhaps the same kind of soil upon which Jacob the Patriarch lay, dreaming of angels and a ladder. And perhaps it was mixed with ashes of the altar from the temple or brought from the place where nuclear waste is dumped. Either way, this soil was not here when I bought the house; it was brought here from elsewhere, no one knows from where exactly, and it has worked miracles.

This is what happened: one day I hired a Bobcat operator to do a few jobs in the garden. A Bobcat is a kind of multipurpose small tractor. Aside from a loader bucket there are all kinds of useful parts that can be attached to it. The Bobcat is wheel driven, but the steering is like that of a crawler. I won't go into further details, but if readers are having difficulty deciding

what to buy me for my next birthday—I can solve the problem: I'd like a Bobcat. I will even make do with a secondhand one.

A Bobcat is an agile, efficient contraption, and the person operating it must be agile and efficient, too. I was glad to discover that the person I had hired that day was a veritable magician. While serving in the military, I learned, he was a helicopter pilot. All the aeronautic coordination he had cultivated in order to fly a helicopter he now demonstrated on the face of the earth. He guided the Bobcat hither and thither, its loader bucket rising and falling as it advanced with the kind of smooth reliable flow that evokes envy and admiration, as it is written: "Seest thou a man diligent in his business? He shall stand before kings." This is the splendor of the Hebrew language: even before the Bobcat existed, the Hebrew language contrived sentences that perfectly describe the person operating the Bobcat.

At a certain stage we needed a few cubic feet of soil. We spoke to a building contractor who was working in one of the neighbors' houses, and he said he would try to find some for me. He was not sure he could do it, so he explained, due to the small quantity we required, but he knew someone who could speak to someone else, who could ask someone to send someone else's cousin, the best friend of a car mechanic who knew someone who owned a truck, and if his partner agreed, he would tell his driver to carry out the task at hand—but only if I paid in advance. I thought about it and decided that if this person was a crook, he would have concocted a simpler and less alluring story than the one he told me. I paid in advance and the next morning awoke to discover that a nice heap of soil had been deposited at the edge of the garden. The Bobcat operator got to work right away, distributing most of the soil between the oak trees in the northwest corner of the garden.

When I began living in the village, this entire corner was overrun with thistles, and aggressive creepers covered most of the treetops, blocking the sun and giving the trees a miserable appearance. I cut down and uprooted the thistles; I trimmed the creepers close to the ground and untangled them from the oak trees with the help of my old pickup truck, ropes, and tow straps.

The trees were extremely happy, recovered swiftly, and grew branches and foliage. This corner quickly became a delightful spot and earned the name *zula,* or "hangout." I planted squill bulbs and honeysuckle there and, after the new soil had been distributed, I sowed buttercups. I must stress that these seeds grew and blossomed in my garden, in other words buttercups I am familiar with and that are known to me, the offspring of perfectly normal buttercups in every way.

Like the seeds of other geophytes, the anemone and cyclamen, gladiolus and squill, buttercup seeds produce small leaflets in their first year that increase in size the following year, and the year after that. Meanwhile the bulbs develop underground and produce their first flowers only after three to four years. But the leaflets that sprouted from the buttercup seeds I sowed back then in that same soil grew voluminously, and the leaves were triple their usual size. In their first year these buttercups were already producing flowers double the size of all the others! Since I knew their parents, I had no doubt that this was not hereditary but due to environmental conditions—namely the soil that had been brought to the garden. I made some inquiries, but could not find out who brought the soil and from where.

For some years the buttercups continued to produce gigantic flowers in the *zula,* but they finally settled down and began producing flowers of a normal size. Today, anything I plant or sow in the *zula* grows as it does in any other place in the garden. That mysterious soil has lost its special powers and is as earthy as the next clump of soil. What was its secret? What did it have that faded away or simply disappeared? I do not know. A riddle it is and a riddle it remains.

26

Collecting and Other Dangers

Years ago, when I began writing my first novel, *The Blue Mountain*, I
met with some of the last pioneers of the Second Aliyah. They were
all over the age of ninety, and the eldest was ninety-six years old. His name
was Eliezar Slotzkin, a member of Ein Harod Ihud Kibbutz. The years had
not blunted his sense of humor, and he enjoyed mocking himself and his
friends.

"I heard you're meeting all the old-timers in the valley," he greeted me
at our first meeting in his room on the kibbutz. "What for? They've no
idea what they're saying anymore."

"What are you talking about, Slotzkin?" I answered him. "You're the
oldest of the whole lot."

"That's true," he said, "but they were already stupid at the age of twenty."

Eliezar Slotzkin was a technical person. "I was just the plumber of Ein
Harod," he told me, "and I used to get jealous when I saw the golden boys
of the kibbutz coming back from the fields." But he made a point of telling
me that he was the one who designed and installed all the plumbing when
the kibbutz was founded.

"And what do you do today?" I asked.

"Today I repair faucets and valves in the kibbutz workshop," he said, adding apologetically, "but only for a few hours a day. Part-time."

"And how do they treat you?"

"They treat me very well," he answered, wearing a look of innocence, "but it's not because they love me that much but because I won't give them the map of the underground pipe system," and Slotzkin burst out laughing. "They can't dig anywhere without first asking me where they can safely use the backhoe loader."

Slotzkin died a few years later at the age of one hundred years and three days. A few of his lines and insights appear in *The Blue Mountain*, and I have not forgotten him. This is not just because of his humor and wisdom, but for another reason: every time I dig the soil in my garden in order to plant or sow, repair a leak, or expose a mole rat's tunnel under mounds of earth—I hit a pipe. I don't understand why or how, but as soon as I thrust a pitchfork or shovel into the ground, or pound it with a rake or pickax—a fountain shoots up into the air. I like to think that God endowed me with a sixth sense for finding underground sources of water. It might not be groundwater, but it's not bad for starters.

Damaging a pipeline is not the only danger inherent in gardening. There are also scorpion burrows, and I have already come across viper and wasp nests, which I will discuss later. But the truth is that I am perfectly capable of damaging myself without any assistance from these fearsome creatures. Almost every time I go out to work in the garden there is a branch that scratches my forehead badly enough for it to bleed, a flowerpot that trips me up, a raffia string that winds itself around my ankles, and I further excel in getting very muddy.

Aware of this talent, I always make sure to wear old, worn work clothing kept precisely for this purpose before setting out for the garden. But it often happens that I return home from one place or another in ordinary clothes, and while walking along the fifty feet of path from road to house I cast a glance to the left to see what has sprouted, or bloomed, or withered, and I always see weeds that need to be uprooted immediately, and as I stoop over them I notice a lupine seedling that ought to be elsewhere, but because I am lazy, and the ground is damp and soft, I poke my fingers in and remove it together with a small clump of soil around its roots. Then I pace across the mud to where I might plant it, and, once there, I go down on my knees absentmindedly, planting the little lupine, and then get up and wipe my hands distractedly on my pants.

A similar thing occurs on summer mornings when I detect bite marks of thirsty jackals on the irrigation pipes. In such a case the pipe should be cut and the offending section removed, and then the pipe should be reattached to a hollow plastic connector. For this reason, the main gate valve must remain closed for a few minutes. I, however, under the influence of neural synapses which determine my level of intelligence but are beyond my understanding, quickly cut the pipe without closing the gate valve.

What happens next has happened before and will happen again: the water bursts out, drenching my eyeglasses, and in this way, half blind, I attempt to assemble the snipped ends of each side of the connector. My wet hands slip on the pipe, the connector flies off, and I get a shower of water mixed with mud on my face and clothes, just like last time.

These are all well-documented and familiar incidents that frequently happen, but they all concern physical dangers and injuries, while the biggest danger lurking at the door of every gardener of the wild is mental: collector's disease. I am describing this as a disease, since it is difficult to recover from yet easy to catch. Usually people catch it because they are particularly interested in a certain subject, and perhaps even wish to learn about it, but after a period of incubation unbeknownst to the person who is infected, and who might even feel healthier than usual, the disease can

be incurable. I speak from personal experience because once, out of the love I have for children's storybooks, I fell ill with this disease, and I well remember the infection, deterioration, addiction, and—to my joy—also the recovery, which happened at the very last moment.

I began writing relatively late, but was already reading at a very young age. I quickly became immersed in it, and then my father told me that in the wooden crate where linens were stored in his mother's house there was treasure to be found: tens of old books, most of them bound in red, from a publishing house known as Omanut Publishers. These books had been read by my father in his own childhood: *A Tale of Two Cities, Huckleberry Finn, Twenty Thousand Leagues Under the Sea, Les Misérables* and *The Hunchback of Notre-Dame, The Talisman, The Voyages of Dr. Dolittle, Three Men in a Boat, In Desert and Wilderness, Montezuma's Daughter, Moon Mountains, The Last Days of Pompeii, The Adventures of Captain Hatteras,* and a host of others.

Whenever we visited my grandmother, she always agreed to let me read one of those books—but when I asked to borrow the book so that I could continue reading it at home, she refused. Perhaps she was worried I wouldn't give the book back or that I would stop visiting her if all the books were handed over to me. But my father, who sensed my disappointment and who wanted me to read copiously, devised a scheme: he would keep her busy with a thing or two that would hold her attention, I would take a book while she wasn't looking, and the next time we visited, I would return that book and take another. This is exactly what we did, and those books, with their plots and heroes and their flowery, outdated translations, were much loved by me and became part of my world. Today I still recall pictures and characters and lines from them: "SIRE, a fresh dispatch," from the opening of *Michael Strogoff,* and "Oh, come and see the skulls; come back and see the skulls!" from the visit to the graveyard in *Three Men in a Boat.* And "Let's have it out with swords, gentlemen, not pins!" from *Tartarin of Tarascon,* and "Captain Hatteras always went northward," and of course "Mr. Holmes, they were the footprints of a gigantic hound!," and the names of all Dr. Dolittle's animals, and so on and so forth.

Some years after my grandmother's death, her apartment was rented out to students, and I also lived there for a few years. I quickly released all the books from their penitentiary and took them for myself, and then I was overcome with a desire to find and purchase more books from Art Publishers in order to complete the entire collection. My desire turned into passion, my passion into an irrepressible urge, and the disease swiftly spread, "dealt with in its most virulent form"—also a quotation from one of the above books, and to demonstrate to you the depth of my addiction— I began to bring home all sorts of other old books, too.

At a certain stage I discovered that I was not interested in the content of the books I procured but rather in their uniqueness: their age and rarity and, even worse, the number of books I owned and the very fact that I owned them. I cultivated relationships with bookdealers and exchanged books with other addicts until one day, while working for the Israel Broadcasting Authority, I found myself fabricating some fiction in order to escape a day of editing and travel from Jerusalem to Haifa because a bookstore owner told me that "a few promising crates" had arrived, adding that if I could get there that same day he would wait for me before displaying the books on his shelves.

I left Jerusalem feeling excited and happy, but this time something happened that had never happened before. While driving, I began wondering what had come over me and what exactly I was doing. At Sha'ar Hagai, this brooding became a weighty conversation with myself; at Latrun I turned the car around, and just as decisively as I quit smoking a few years later, I cured myself that very day of collector's disease. I stopped buying books I did not need and even sold or gave away some of the books in my collection. I still own a large library today, but all the books are either ones I enjoy rereading or require for work.

There are also certain features of collecting in the growing of wildflowers, but of a completely different sort: a person who collects books, stamps, old work utensils, corsets of Spanish queens, Victorian coal irons, hoods and valves of Duesenberg automobiles, Belgian wall clocks from the eighteenth century, and train schedules from the Austro-Hungarian Empire knows that none of these items has the ability to reproduce. Even if we do not know exactly how many there are, the number is finite, and the collector strives to discover as many as possible and to procure them, to derive pleasure not only because he owns them but because other collectors do not.

Wildflowers, on the other hand, are living organisms and can be grown and made to multiply rather than merely collected. I have met growers on several occasions who endeavor to amass in their gardens every single type of plant growing in Israel, or at least every type of sage and every variation of clover. However, people like myself who are simply lovers of nature, who are not collectors or professional botanic gardeners and who do not want to be inscribed in the *Guinness Book of World Records*, simply grow flowers they love and enjoy the beauty therein.

I certainly enjoy detailing the list of wild plants that grow in my garden, but this is not the main point or purpose. It is their beauty that is important, greater in my eyes than that of ornamental flowers, the engagement with and knowledge that can be gleaned from them, the thoughts and love these flowers arouse within me, their very existence as a collection that lives, breathes, eats, drinks, and reproduces, rather than a collection of dead items imprisoned in boxes and drawers. Most of all, I revel in the knowledge that there will always be a collection that is larger and richer than mine, larger and richer in fact than any collection belonging to gardeners who are better and more devoted than I—nature itself, where all these plants evolved and where they can be found today.

27

The Great Snapdragon

One day, traveling from Jerusalem to Tel Aviv, I noticed on the northern verges of the highway, a little after the Shoresh interchange, that genocide was about to occur. The victims were wild plants I knew and loved: an established group of great snapdragons that flowered at the beginning of every summer in a wonderful purple array, bringing joy to travelers on the road or, more accurately, bringing joy to those whose hearts were receptive to such things and took notice.

The great snapdragon is the father of the cultivated snapdragon, which blooms in a variety of colors in gardens and squares, and I have been told that they also crossbreed. Botanists are deeply horrified by such crossbreeding, because they are punctilious with regard to the purity of race and species. I certainly understand them, but secretly I admit that this crossbreeding arouses an excitement of the literary type within me, such as one finds in Jack London's stories about crossbreeding dogs with wolves, and theories of researchers into human evolution on the likelihood of mating between *Homo sapiens* and Neanderthals, particularly in Greek mythological stories about human-animal hybrids.

It is not only the great snapdragon that has cultivated versions but also the poppy, buttercup, and cyclamen. They are larger and, in my opinion, unsightly and rougher than their wild matriarchs. The same thing is true of cultivated tulips that are treated with additional colors until they resemble plastic flowers in both shape and hue.

The Madonna lily that flowers in my garden is the mother of lilies that are not exclusively white but also pink and yellowish and have lost some of their lovely fragrance through this unnatural selection. All these flowers, to my mind, are comparable to ridiculous types of lap dogs and fancy cats—all kinds of Siamese cyclamens and Angora poppies. To my great relief, the cultivated squill has yet to be invented, but that will happen, as things do, and then we will have a short, fat squill that will flower by springtime in yellow and pink.

Either way, what was threatening this group of great snapdragons was the widening of the road leading to Jerusalem, preparations for which had just begun. Measurements had been taken, and the heavy machinery had already arrived. The great snapdragon does not have a bulb or tuber that can be transplanted from place to place, but luckily all this happened a little after the flowers began blossoming. I managed to gather up some seeds there, and that very autumn I sowed them in my garden.

As happens with most of my wildflowers, I expected the great snapdragon to sprout after the rain, to grow during winter, and to flower in spring. However, it did not sprout at all, not even one of its seeds. I wondered if something about the garden was bothering it. I even felt happy that, like the plants themselves, I had reserved a few seeds—think of it as a kind of sperm bank—that I stored in a jar and the plants stored under the soil.

Meanwhile, the snapdragon continued to behave strangely in my garden: winter passed, and not one seed sprouted. Spring passed and nothing happened. And then, the snapdragon seeds surprised me by sprouting precisely in the middle of summer! At the hottest and driest time of the year, fresh little green sprouts rose up in the garden. Sometimes seeds sprout out of season in the watered berms that circle my pomegranate and citrus trees, but these seeds sprouted in a completely dry area. At first I did not recognize them, but because I wanted to find out who these unfamiliar, unexpected guests were, I watered them with a watering can for two to three weeks until they grew a little more, and then I realized it was the snapdragon I had rescued from the Jerusalem–Tel Aviv highway.

The surprises did not stop here. Rather than flowering in April on stalks almost three feet high, my snapdragon flowered in January on very short stalks. I asked it the meaning of such behavior; the dragon neither snapped back at me nor roared an answer. I gathered the new seeds it produced and sowed them the following autumn. Since then my snapdragons sprout at the right time, and they blossom and roar as usual. It could be that they had been suffering from a little jet lag or were just overcome by a pleasant dizziness, the same way I suffered when I left Jerusalem and came to live here. Either way, if anyone is wondering what happened to the great snapdragon that once flowered along the verges of the highway leading to Jerusalem, not far from the moshav of Shoeva—well, today they flower in the Jezreel Valley, and all is well with them.

28

Kramer the Cat

There is also a grave in the garden, reminding me that not only life, sprouting, and flowering, colors, and fragrances, but also death is present here. I am not referring to the predictable death of annual plants, which sprout at winter's onset, bloom at its end, create seeds, and wither in summer, nor am I referring to what looks like death but is merely a kind of hibernation of bulbs and tubers, but a surprising death, an irreversible one, that strikes suddenly and causes pain.

I have had several deaths like this in the garden: the demise of my lemon tree, more of which I will tell later; the chinaberry's execution, of which I have already spoken; and the death of my beloved cat, Kramer the Cat, who presided unchallenged over the garden while alive, and who is buried here today.

Kramer was about a year old when I got him, and he lived with me for eleven years. He spent most of his days sleeping deeply, as I described in the first of three children's books I wrote about him. Kramer had a heart that remained awake while sleeping, not for romantic reasons but for tactical ones—even while sleeping he watched over the garden lest a dog or stray cat wander into it.

Kramer loved sleeping and he was good at it. Aside from his favorite snooze spots inside the house, he also had a few in the garden. His most beloved spot was in the shade of the buckthorn, close to the Madonna lilies and verbena bush. At first, I thought he had chosen this particular spot because of the agreeable fragrances of the two. Then one day I decided to investigate exactly what he was doing there. I laid myself down and realized just how calculating a cat he was: from where he lay, Kramer could see most of the area between the house and the street and the entire length of the garden path, from street to front door. When I opened the door, I could see him lying there, and he always opened his eyes, and we would exchange looks and yowls, but those coming from the street into the garden could not see him until he stood up.

If the visitor was a mere human, Kramer ignored his presence. If the person was familiar, Kramer would get up to greet him. If it was a dog or cat, he would charge at it without forewarning. Both escaped immediately, but unlike the cats, who simply turned around and fled, the dogs also yowled with terror, which greatly amused both of us.

Nothing about Kramer's appearance hinted at such aggressiveness. He was a large cat, black from the tip of his tail to the end of his nose, but fluffy and plump and altogether affable. He did not appear significantly energetic or of athletic capabilities. Neither did he belong to the common variety of cats who bring home gifts in the form of butchered lizards or dismembered birds. All these little creatures were beneath his dignity, but when he spied a rat or snake, he would leap valiantly into action: hastening home to call on me to take care of the problem.

He had a special way of calling me in these cases, one of a number of cries and gestures that I learned to decipher: the one that said "I want to go out," the ones that said "I want to come in," "I want food," and "I'm not enjoying this," and the most special one, the beseeching one, which cried, "Let's go home. I don't want to go to the vet." That sentence, by the way, was said in a single word that repeated itself the entire journey to the veterinary clinic, the word "gaaooooo." In my opinion, when Kramer died, it was not merely a wonderful cat that disappeared but the last vestiges of a rare breed of cat able to pronounce the consonant *g*.

K ramer died from kidney failure leading to multiple organ dysfunction. During his last days he was hospitalized by his personal physician, Dr. Yair Ben-Tzioni, who made every possible effort to save Kramer. At the end, when it became evident that nothing would help and that Kramer was in obvious pain, I asked Dr. Ben-Tzioni to put him to sleep.

As mentioned, I buried Kramer under the buckthorn, near the Madonna lilies and verbena, a place where he loved to fall asleep while on duty. Whenever I pass by this spot, a few times a day, I remember and miss his presence. The relationship between us was one of love and understanding, and every morning when I open the front door, I wonder why Kramer does not emerge from his little sleeping box—at night he preferred sleeping outside, by the front door—to stretch before entering the house.

Kramer was the first cat I ever had and—in the meanwhile—the only one. When he died, the news spread swiftly through the village, and by the next day a few cats had showed up for an audition, hoping to take Kramer's place. But cats are creatures who differ from one another much more than dogs, and I could not find a worthy candidate to take Kramer's place in my heart and home. Some of them were more beautiful than he was, most of them were more alert, but not one of them was Kramer. They say that everyone is replaceable, but it seems to me that this is simply not true when it comes to Kramer.

29

Splendid Bindweed

*S*ummer guests are always disappointed.

   "Is this your garden?" they exclaim.

"Everything's dry. There's nothing here," they add, pointing to the neighbors' manicured garden, a garden of grass and sprinklers, cultivated flowers and stylized stone walls, and a professional gardener who designed and planted and sowed and who now is responsible for its upkeep: pruning and mowing, improving improvements, gathering and disposing of leaves, programming the computerized irrigation system.

"It really is a lovely garden," I say, "but my garden is a wild one. It's green in winter, and after that it's red and yellow and blue and pink and purple and white, and now it's summertime and everything is dry."

But the truth is that in summer a wild garden is not a total loss. The visitors I have already mentioned flower and flourish here: all sorts of nosy people and those who fancy themselves to be experts and who look upon me with compassion.

Aside from that, the trees are green in summer as well, and I also have a few heroic flowers, invincible ones, that laugh at aridity and jeer at heat. I appreciate their strength and envy their stamina. It is easy to prosper and bloom and produce fruit in season when you are planted on the banks of a stream and the spring sun caresses your chlorophyll, but spring passes, clouds disperse, the sun blazes and scorches. Water evaporates, the ground cracks, and signs of impending death are discernible on most of the plants: their heads are bowed, their petals fall, the green grows pale, the yellow spreads and takes over. It is actually now that everything around withers, the virgin's bower, the lily, the squill, and the splendid bindweed. This last one is worthy of being recognized and grown in every garden in Israel, both because of its beauty and also because of its tolerance to dryness and heat.

Splendid bindweed can be seen in the months of May and June, when it blossoms on the Menashe Hills, on the pathways of the Lower Galilee, the inner coastal region, and the Golan Heights: low, globular shrubs, resplendent with small flowers in pink and purple. Its dense and beautiful blossoms can last right through to the beginning of July, and in good years the last of its flowers can be seen changing the guard with the first of the squills. The splendid bindweed is truly spellbinding: the eye is drawn to its lovely color, and the heart thanks the flower for the effort and strength required to blossom precisely in this difficult season.

Wherein lies the bindweed's secret power? Unfortunately, I am no expert botanist, nor have I carried out scientific research into the acclimation of plants to dryness and heat. Even an amateur such as I, however, can discern that the bindweed produces leaves in winter and sheds them in summer. In this way, it prevents loss of water through the surface of the leaves. But the true blessing lies in what is hidden from the eye: tremendous roots are concealed under the bindweed's delicate-looking canopy, whose structure and breadth allow for the storage of water and nutrients, enabling it to reach deep, moisture-laden layers even in summer.

I have a few bindweed plants in the garden. Two of them I saved from an area that was being dug up and turned into a reservoir on the Menashe Hills. The rest I sowed and grew myself. As I have already mentioned, I gathered these seeds on the verges of Highway 6, where many of the bindweed's brethren were planted and which were breathtaking to behold. Regretfully, one day they all vanished. What a loss this is.

One way or another, I placed the seeds I had gathered in small pots, and after a few of them had germinated, I transplanted them to their permanent place in the soil. This may sound easy, but the bindweed is difficult to germinate and grow. Only a few seeds germinated, and only a few of those developed and strengthened, and I hope I also manage to convey the sense of time here, because years passed before the bindweed I had sown grew and flowered.

Suffice to say, I planted some of them in partial shade because I wanted to make it a little easier for them to cope with the sun and its harsh radiation. To my surprise, I discovered that the ones planted in full sunlight grew faster and flowered more profusely. I transplanted their brothers there as well—and now they are happy and give thanks the only way a plant can: they flower beautifully under the sun year after year, making do with the minimum and coping easily with the harsh Israeli summer, free of the need to be watered. Dewdrops and minimal moisture stored in the depths of the soil are enough for this plant to withstand any drought, water companies, or heat waves.

Since they do so well under difficult conditions, I decided to leave the fertilization and reproduction entirely in their hands. This is why I do not gather their seeds, nor do I sow them myself. They drop their seeds to the ground, and I have already come across new offspring alongside the more established plants—in other words, if one day someone decides to restore the bindweed to Highway 6, I will be able to give them seeds from the original bindweed that once grew there.

30

Cracked Olives

I have several olive trees in my garden. As I explained earlier—these are young trees, their yield is small and does not warrant going to an olive press. Until such time as they grow taller and bear more fruit, I harvest a few buckets every year and pickle them deliciously. When is the right time to harvest the olives? Some say this is after the first rain, because it causes the olives to swell. Others say the first rain simply washes off the dust. There are also those who claim that olives should be harvested when they begin to blacken. I harvest them when I think they are nicely plump, mottled with pale spots, and when—I admit—I have time.

I also prepare black olives, and these I harvest when they are worthy of their description—in other words, when they have blackened. This is an opportunity to correct a common error: black olives and green ones are not two different varieties, as is the case with black muscat Hamburg grapes and their white counterparts, muscat of Alexandria. A green olive is the unripe fruit, and the black olive is the ripened one. If you have the time and inclination, you are welcome to choose a tree bearing olives and to stretch out in its shade for a few weeks. By not removing your gaze from the tree, you will be able to see the olives blackening before your very eyes.

Pickling olives is a masculine art, or at least that's what men think. Perhaps they think this because in the past it was customary to crack olives using a stone, with all the Neanderthal connotations attached to that, and perhaps because the Hebrew language is fond of the word for "pickle"—*kibush,* the root of which means "conquer" and which is used in all sorts of male domains. Admittedly, I mentioned here the path conquered by the poet Rachel's feet, but Rachel is the exception that proves the rule: Hebrew conquers the land, conquers women, conquers ways, conquers instincts, conquers a person imprisoned or enslaved, and if there is still strength, it also conquers olives.

The truth is that it is very easy to both conquer and pickle olives. Even my father—who kept his distance from ovens, cooking pots and pans, and the kitchen in general, and who never cooked or baked or fried or preserved—would buy a few pounds of olives in the market every year and pickle them in a jar, and like all the other males took great pride in this. Note well: aside from salt and garlic and lemon and hot pepper, men put into their jar of olives the added ingredient of competition. A man who gives his buddy a jar of pickled olives made with his own bare hands— "the work of his hands that he may be glorified" might be a more fitting description here—does not do it merely out of friendship or generosity, but to make it perfectly clear that his olives are better than the other man's.

Once, in a vegetable store in a nearby Arab village, I chanced upon a conversation with my own kind about the pickling of olives. The grocer was offering tastes of olives he had pickled himself and that were for sale. He glanced sideways at his interlocutors with a patronizing look reserved for precisely a moment like this, and the customers—both Jews and Arabs—tasted the olives, exchanged similar looks with the grocer, and began bestowing advice and suggesting suggestions.

I also tasted the olives and, like everyone else, was happy to discover that my pickled olives were better than the grocer's. Not that this was news to me. Like every male, I also know how to pickle olives better than any other man. "Very tasty," I told him respectfully and as a matter of course offered my own suggestions on how to improve his olives so that they would reach the unattainable level of mine.

Theoretically, these suggestions are trade secrets. But we, the conquering males of olives, do not keep our recipes a secret. On the contrary, we are happy to divulge to any rookie who asks, knowing with certainty that his olives will never be as good as our own. For this reason, I will gladly divulge my own recipe, a simple and basic one intended for those who shy away from various special additions and pungent herbs which, as with cooking in general, conceal the good taste of the fundamental ingredients.

I'll begin with the olives themselves. There are purists who refuse to pickle olives they did not pick with their own hands from an organic tree they grew themselves or whose grower they know intimately. I respect their way, but I will not join them. Those who do not have their own olives to pick can purchase them in the market, at least here in Israel. Of course, it's worth inspecting the olives to make sure they are firm and plump and beautiful rather than mere gaunt flesh, flaccid and blemished, but this rule applies to all fruits and vegetables.

I rinse black olives in water, and while they are drying I take empty bottles of mineral water, cut and remove their bases, upturn and fill them with layer upon layer of sea salt and olives. Once the bottles are filled, I stand them upside down on old newspapers in a shady place. The salt absorbs and soaks up moisture from the olives, and any surplus drips through the spout and is sopped up by the newspaper. After ten days, I taste them, changing the brine if necessary, and then continue the process for a few more days. Then I rinse the salt from the olives, place them in jars, submerge them in olive oil, seal, and the next day they are ready.

There is another method I myself have never tried, but I've heard about it, and it sounds like a good one. Apparently, it is perfect for small black olives. Soak them in brine for several months in sealed containers, then strain, pour olive oil over them, and by the next day you will be able to slice bread, add a selection of salami, green cucumber, tomato, salty cheese, open a bottle of arak, and invite friends. Your friends will taste them, praise you, say the olives are pretty good, but they heard from a grandfather or an uncle or an old shepherd they met in the Galilee that it's worthwhile adding aniseed, rue, cumin, hyssop, and various other misfortunes to the pickling mixture and let them age in an oak pickling barrel. But everyone knows none of this will do any good, because of the basic principle that cannot be concealed or undercut: your own olives are always superior.

As for green olives, soak them in water for several days. Change the water every couple of days and then water the plants with it. After soaking, you must make a decision: whole or cracked, also referred to as "slit open." The main difference between the pickling of whole or cracked olives is how long the process takes. Cracked olives are ready for consumption within a few weeks, whereas whole olives are ready only after a few months. Exactly how many? Open the jar and try one.

How are olives cracked? Well then, there are fundamentalists who strike olive after olive with a stone or wooden hammer. This process takes up a good deal of time and splatters drops, one of which—always!—enters the eye of the hammerer, who then issues a cry loud enough to warrant a response from a chorus of jackals. There is always the option of going to the market and looking for the man with the special gadget for this kind of thing. The perfectionists, the elite pickle makers, make a slit in each olive and talk about it incessantly while serving the olives to guests. I am in the habit of putting handful after handful into a thick nylon bag, the type used to collect waste from building sites, and to thrash them amicably with a stick or heavy frying pan.

Once the olives have been cracked, broken, or slit, boil water in order to dissolve the salt and create a solution within which the olives can marinate in jars. Much importance is placed on the concentration of the solution, because aside from the taste it gives, the salt preserves the olives for a long period of time. Too little and the olives will be ragged and tasteless; too much and they will be inedible.

The nostalgic types determine the amount of salt using an egg plunged into the brine. This tradition was begun by their grandfather's grandfather, who owned an olive stall in Odessa or was the official egg plunger of Sultan Abed el-Khamid. Either way, the egg must float between the surface of the liquid and the bottom of the jar. If there is not enough salt, the egg will sink to the bottom, and if there is too much, it will bob up in the water like an iceberg. This anecdote, which appears in cookery columns attempting an air of earthiness and authenticity, is misleading. To be more precise, it only works when the egg is really fresh, laid by your own hen straight into the palm of your hand. Eggs that have spent time in refrigerated trucks and storage facilities lose fluid, suffer from air bubbles, and float like water wings.

In short, instead of floating eggs, I taste the brine, add water or salt if necessary, and adhere to this simple rule: it must be a littler saltier than seawater. I know this sounds somewhat strange and vague, but if you try it you will discover that this simple and practical piece of advice also works when pickling cucumbers.

Now wait for the brine to cool down a little. Meanwhile, arrange the olives and the rest of the ingredients in a jar or plastic container that has been thoroughly cleaned and dried and which has a hermetically sealed lid. Place a few slices of lemon at the bottom of the jar or container, add peeled garlic cloves and hot peppers, and over this a layer of olives that reaches a third or a quarter of the way up the jar—each pickle maker to his own—and over this another layer of lemon, garlic, and hot pepper. Pour in the brine and then enough olive oil to reach the top of the jar, seal, and store in a dark place.

A few days later shake the jar and shake it again. Then open it and taste the brine with a teaspoon, correcting what needs correcting: I add salt or water, occasionally a little garlic, hot pepper, or fresh lemon juice, and after a further month I taste and correct again. That's it. From here onward, let time take its course until one day you taste the olives, discover they are ready, and quickly invite friends around. Enjoy a sense of fulfillment and take no notice of any advice your friends offer or any comments they make. Your olives will be superior to theirs, but inferior to mine.

31

Two Moons of Sowing

In Hebrew, the word *zera* means both "seed" and "semen," and indeed semen is referred to in the Bible as "seed." But a plant seed is not a male cell but a body that contains a fetus and all the nutrients needed at its inception. Animal fetuses develop and are nourished within eggs and wombs until either hatched or born. Many of them continue to be cared for and protected and nourished long after that time. In the case of humans, this may even continue past the age of thirty. Plant seeds, on the other hand, have no one to look after them, show concern for them or feed them as they ripen and germinate, nor as they grow. They are dumped into the world together with a personal Spartan survival kit: some kind of a protective shell, a living tissue that will produce roots and cotyledons—as the first leaflets are known—and nutrients for the beginning of their lives, until the roots begin to absorb and the leaflets to photosynthesize and produce glucose. They are further endowed with incredible resilience, unsurpassed patience and a capability that many attribute to animals: to sense environmental conditions and to behave and respond in accordance with them.

To this end, the plant seed possesses sensors and measuring devices:

a thermometer, hygrometer, a rain gauge, and in my humble opinion, a clock as well. The seed sprouts only after the measurements have convinced it that there is a chance of completing an entire cycle of life: to germinate and grow and blossom and multiply and produce new seeds. And there is another manifestation of prudent planning: even in good conditions, not all seeds in the soil will sprout. Even someone who lacks a botanic education knows that not all lupines planted as seeds in the garden will sprout, nor every hollyhock. As though they are thinking ahead, these plants save reserve duty seeds in the soil. This is the sperm bank I mentioned in one of the earlier chapters.

The seeds undergo a period of waiting between their ripening and the first rain. Anemone seeds, for example, wait a few months, whereas squill seeds only wait a few weeks. Both the anemone and the squill lie exactly where they fall, regardless of whether this is the ideal spot for growing and sprouting. They are subject to the vagaries of heat and cold, gusts of wind, fluxes of water, trampling feet, voracious mouths or beaks, and many of them perish during this period of time. But in my garden, despite the fact that I proudly refer to it as "wild," the seeds enjoy a shelter and protection that they would never receive in the real wild—me.

Every year I gather the seeds of my wildflowers and put them aside in my house until autumn, in either a paper envelope or an open jar—which is crucial—since seeds go moldy when kept in closed containers. After the first decent rains have fallen, I sow the seeds in what seems like a good place. It is possible, indeed, to let nature take its course and, like the seeds themselves, hope for divine providence. But when I choose the exact spot, secreting them away under the soil properly, the sprouting percentage and success rate increase, and the relationship between the seeds and me deepens and ameliorates.

In order for all this to happen, the seeds must be gathered and stored before they fall to the ground or fly through the air, attach themselves to fur or socks, or get eaten and excreted somewhere else. There are plants, such as the lupine or great snapdragon, whose fruit must be scrutinized on a daily basis and quickly gathered the moment it ripens; otherwise the seeds will swiftly scatter. There are plants whose seeds remain a part of them for much longer, such as Agrostemma, hollyhock, sea squill, hyacinth squill, gladiolus, crocus, and, particularly, the buttercup. And there are plants somewhere in the middle of all these, such as the Syrian cornflower-thistle and the anemone.

The most demanding of all is the poppy. Its minuscule seeds develop within flower capsules, the likes of which I have already described. Capsules of different plants have different shapes—the flower capsule of the poppy looks like an inverted bell with a circular lid that seals its inner compartments. As the poppy capsules mature, their outer layer turns from greenish to yellowish and even light brown, and consequently tiny vents develop under and around the rim, and when the poppy stalks sway in the wind, the seeds spill out through the vents, spilling onto the ground the same way salt pours from a saltshaker, close to the parent plant. This is how the poppy creates those wonderful red fields in the countryside.

The poppy fruit does not ripen all at the same time. On any one poppy plant, green buds that have not yet bloomed can be seen alongside red blossoms (each flower blossoms for a single day), withered flowers whose petals have fallen, and the green capsules whose seeds have yet to mature, and the yellowing ones whose vents are already exposed. This is why the poppy grower must scour his garden on a daily basis and harvest any capsules that have ripened.

Harvesting the poppies is a delicate task. Every touch to the plant disperses seeds, and they are so tiny that some of them spill like water, overflowing on every slope like water, slippery as water, and—again like water—if the seeds fall to the ground, they cannot be gathered, in exactly the way the wise woman of Tekoa described another irreversible process in Samuel 2: "For we must needs die, and *are* as water spilt on the ground, which cannot be gathered up again."

This is why I equip myself with scissors, grasp the capsule gently, cut the stem, taking care it does not incline either to the left or right, and definitely not downward, and place it in a bucket, where it can scatter seeds to its heart's content. The problem is that this only works if you have two or three poppies in your garden, but when you have tens or even hundreds of them—we all want brides and grooms having their photos taken in our garden—you must visit them daily, search out the ripened fruits, grasp them, cut them, take care, and then return the next day to see if any more have ripened, an activity that wastes much time.

Perhaps this is more suited to the offspring of nobility, lacking purpose, surrounded by chambermaids and servants, rather than those who have work to do.

I finally found a solution: when the poppies begin to ripen, I roll out nylon sheets over several square feet and place a few stones at the edges to keep the sheets from flying away. Whenever I notice plants whose flowers have already wilted and whose fruit has mostly mellowed, I carefully uproot them, neither shaking nor tilting. Then, with bated breath, I go over to the nylon sheet and place the plant there as though it were a newborn in a cradle.

In this way, a whole host of poppy plants accumulates and dries on the sheet. From time to time I turn them over gently, and finally I remove them, folding and gathering the corners of the sheet and pouring the seeds and dry leaves and particles of soil that have accumulated upon it into a large plastic bathtub. I then put them through a *kevara,* and then a *naffa,* and finally transfer them to a jar using a strainer and a funnel, and there the seeds will lie through summer, until they are sowed the following autumn.

The cyclamen also stores its seeds inside a capsule, but it resembles a ball in shape. It similarly ripens over several weeks, forcing me to visit frequently and to harvest each capsule precisely before it opens. By now I have learned to recognize the early signs of this: the capsule becomes soft to the touch, the pedicel is thin and flaccid. I pick it, along with the entire stipe, so that it will continue providing nutrients for a few more days. I place it in a flat, open container to enable the capsule to open and the seeds to fall away.

The Syrian cornflower-thistle does not ripen all at once either. Unlike the poppy, its seeds are in no hurry to fall, and they need not be handled with such care, but still it is better to harvest them before they drop to the ground. The Syrian cornflower-thistle ripens spores of fruit that resemble delicate pine cones in hues of yellow and gray, padded with a variety of stalks and husks. To separate the husk from the seeds, I crush them under a large wooden rolling pin: I scatter the dry spores on the marble kitchen counter, pass the rolling pin over them until the seeds pop out, and then drop them into a bowl.

The Agrostemma is more user-friendly. It stores its seeds for an extended period of time in capsules, and harvesting can wait until all the capsules have ripened. Its stems are strong; pulling at the capsule might rip out the entire plant. It is better to snip them with scissors and place them in a bucket. Once—I swear this happened—I was asked by a guest if the same scissors used to cut Agrostemma might also be used to cut poppy stalks. Out of concern that someone else may be worried by this question, I will answer it here: Yes. Poppy and Agrostemma stalks may be cut with the same pair of scissors. They can also be used to cut buttercups, packets of Turkish coffee, pearl barley, and pasta, as well as raffia cord and small cable ties. The larger type of cable tie is best cut with pruning shears, which can also be used to cut the branches of all kinds of trees and sprinkler pipes. Gardening is not a religion. It is all right to use common sense, to improvise, to update, to avoid ridiculous measures, and primarily to enjoy it.

The Agrostemma, meaning "field garland"—and I wonder why this beauty was never given a Hebrew name—is a spectacular perennial that has almost vanished from the Israeli landscape due to the expansion of agriculture. It has a long and delicate stalk and reaches a height of more than thirty inches, ending in two or three purple-pink flowers. When the first Agrostemma plants ripened in my garden I emptied their capsules into a bowl, one by one, with careful fingers. Under the rough outer shell, I discovered a fragile inner sac containing the seeds. I exposed the sac

and then removed it; I rubbed it between thumb and finger, and the seeds dropped into the bowl.

I smiled to myself: I got my first Agrostemma seeds from the Botanical Gardens of the Hebrew University. The workers counted a dozen seeds into the palm of my hand; for me it was as if they were counting diamonds. Wonderfully, this rare and endangered plant has given me back a hundredfold, and I quickly realized that if I were to continue giving personal attention to every single capsule, I would have no time for anything other than seeds of Agrostemma, cyclamen, and poppy. After some thought and a modicum of experimentation, I discovered that the rolling pin works well here, too. I scatter the dry capsules on a marble slab and roll the rolling pin over them (hereby announcing that the same rolling pin can be used to roll pizza dough and Syrian cornflower-thistle), activating moderate physical strength. The seeds pop out with alacrity.

Buttercup seeds are the easiest. They are not trapped inside the fruit but exposed and are well aligned to their stems most of the summer. In their honor I wear rough work gloves to rub the spores forcefully between my hands, and they break loose and fall into a bowl that awaits them on the table.

I try to carry out all these strange tasks when there is no one else in the vicinity. Through the years, I have discovered that they arouse curiosity in others, but after their curiosity is piqued, only criticism and ridicule follow. People always have something to say, not just about the waste of time—Why don't you do something instead of messing about with those dry thorns of yours?—but also about how primitive this task is. It is true that compared with advanced and sophisticated Israeli agriculture, I work in the garden using methods that even Chalcolithic farmers would term outdated.

"When I was a young girl" (I have put this in quotation marks because this is a family saying used by us all, even the males), when milking was done with bare hands, and on Nahalal primary-school trips to neighboring Arab villages, we could still see peasant farmers separating the grain from the chaff with a threshing board, and winnowing with a wooden pitchfork like Araunah the Jebusite in the Book of Samuel and Boaz in the Book of Ruth. I went back to see this after the Six-Day War in villages in the West Bank, and here and there it continues in Eastern Europe to this day. I am not, however, a farmer, but rather a modest grower of wildflowers that are not intended for sale or consumption. I enjoy the extended manual labor, the simplicity and monotony of harvesting, threshing, storing in the granary, and sowing. It fills my head with thoughts and plans, my fingers with memories and knowledge, my heart with hope and confidence. In truth, my seeds will not save me from hunger, nor will they feed me a bounty of bread. They will not fill my granary, larder, or wallet, but there is something relaxing and pleasant in jars full of seeds that may be less than purposeful but tell me that next year my garden will bloom with flowers. That, too, is important.

32

Patience

When I began gathering and storing and sowing seeds from the wildflowers in my garden, I would drop a note into each jar with the name of the plant written on it. I have no need of this today. I recognize every plant I grow not only by its flowers but by a single leaf, fruit, bulb, tuber, or even a seed. Poppy seeds are black or brown, the smallest of my seeds. The great snapdragon's seeds are very similar to the poppy's, except that the black is blacker and they are slightly larger in size. The anemone seeds appear as dark specks wrapped in a pale, fluffy casing, designed to lift them up a little in the wind. Buttercup seeds resemble plump golden flakes, exposed and dense and attached to the tip of the stem where the flower previously was.

The squill seeds similarly resemble small flat flakes, but are glossy black in color. The Syrian cornflower-thistle's seeds are yellowy blue and slippery to the touch. Flax seeds are smaller, darker, and browner than the Syrian cornflower-thistle's, but also slippery and conspicuously oily. Hollyhock seeds are flat, round, and coarse. Lupine seeds are large and hard and flattened, and their colors range from dark brown to yellow and occasionally have a faint pink tinge. The Agrostemma seeds are dark and spherical. Cyclamen seeds are slightly smaller and do not have a single defined shape but look like tiny pebbles colored brown-purple. Even after they completely dry, cyclamen seeds still retain a faint echo of the sweet fragrance they had while still inside the fruit. Gladiolus and crocus seeds are purple and closely resemble each other. I know how to identify all these seeds through the glass of the jar in which they are placed, and today I only need to write the year of harvesting, because plant seeds lose their vitality as the years go by, particularly the tiny seeds of annuals.

After the first rain—if early and bountiful—I break up the soil with a cultivator and uproot the wild weeds that have sprouted, and then I sow my wildflowers, each in its own place. Geophyte seeds—cyclamen, anemone, buttercup, hollyhock, and crocus—I plant in pots and window boxes. I fill them with potting soil up to two-thirds full, scatter the seeds, and add a thin layer of soil over all this. Only after two or three years do I transfer the bulbs and tubers that have developed to a permanent place in the garden.

I sow the seeds of the perennial flowers in the garden itself, but the significant and fundamental difference between this and the sowing of the geophytes, those with a tuber or bulb, is not a technical or agricultural difference but an emotional one. I sow perennials such as poppy, Syrian cornflower-thistle, and lupine in the knowledge that they will recompense me by blooming in a few months—and then dying a few weeks after that. When sowing cyclamen, however, I know it will only bloom a few years from now, but from that time forth it will constantly flower and live longer than I. All this is to say that alongside instant gratification—I'm not denigrating it; instant gratification can be very nice—is also the need for patience.

I am always happy to come across squill bulbs uprooted by a backhoe loader as a road is widened, or when the regional council announces that a hill about to be covered in cement and asphalt can be plundered and

mature cyclamen bulbs removed. But I experience a completely different kind of enjoyment when sowing these flowers and knowing there are no shortcuts. I must obey the rules and regulations of nature and wait several years for the flowers to bloom.

This patience is not something I brought to the garden but rather something I received from it. You could say that I grow plants in the garden, and the garden grows patience in me. This state of mind is a good one, because I am not always patient or willing to wait. There are people and situations that make me short-tempered enough for others to sense it. But the work of writing, which I began late, and the work of gardening, which I began even later, taught me that there are processes that cannot and should not be forced. Among other components and conditions that they require, time itself is of the essence. This is so pronounced that sometimes I think the plants require a hefty dose of time as much as they require water and light.

This is how I learn to wait for the young tree saplings I planted as they gradually grow beside me, and the bulbs that must develop and grow before they produce flowers, and the seeds that will not sprout until their internal clocks tell them to. This is exactly how I wait for a story that needs to ripen slowly, to get accustomed to its protagonists, to become familiar with the storyteller, and the words that must get used to the plot they are forming and even neighboring words with whom they share a page. All these need blocks of time, which translates into patience for the gardener.

There are a few other points of similarity between writing and gardening. Both contain seeds that wait for years in the ground and only sprout, if at all, after the right kind of rain falls. And both of them, if they sprout well, offer beauty, and behind their beauty is much donkeywork: weeding and uprooting, sifting and pruning. And both can lead to back pain, which hates both prolonged periods of sitting at a desk and stooping over plants in a garden. It is a pity I cannot write the way I weed, crawling on all fours.

33

Barefoot

Much of my time in the garden is spent barefoot. Not when it is dark, of course, and not at the height of winter, or when I am using the power scythe or digging with a pitchfork or shovel. But when I go down to my wild garden to see if the flax is blooming? The squill budding? Or to gather seeds and trim shoots that have grown around tree trunks? Perhaps to look for and repair leaks and bird pecks in pipes? Then I wander around barefoot, and I like it very much.

Most people I know are incapable of walking barefoot on the earth, nor do they wish to. People even wear shoes while walking on the beach. It is true that caution should be exercised so as not to tread on broken glass bottles, dog poop, and other treasures concealed in the sand, but usually modern man is afraid, abstaining from unmediated contact with the earth not merely out of caution but as another expression of the sterility that has penetrated our lives in all kinds of ways and through all kinds of doors.

This is also expressed through the Hebrew language. The word *yachef*, "barefoot," is a neutral word, but the word *yachfan*, which comes from the same root, not only means "barefoot person" but also "vagrant": *yachef* is a current situation; *yachfanut*, "vagrancy," is a syndrome, and anyone possessing that syndrome grew up in the semantic field of paupers, idlers, irresponsible people, and also a certain sense of anarchy. In other words, the reluctance to walk barefoot also stems from considerations of one's public image connected to poverty, deviance, and inferiority. Perhaps this is because, in days gone by, only the rich could afford shoes and because prisoners and deportees were sent barefoot to their fates. King David, who could afford to buy his own shoes, and likely had three or four pairs at the least, demonstrated this when he fled from Absalom, his rebel son. King David ascended the Mount of Olives in a show of mourning and wretchedness, "and wept as he went up, and had his head covered, and he went barefoot."

The prophet Isaiah once removed his shoes and went barefoot. He did so in order to attract attention, to elucidate the exile that Assyria intended for Egypt and Kush. This is also evident in God's famous command to Moses: "Put off thy shoes from off thy feet, for the place whereon thou standest is holy ground"—and as such is an expression of humiliation: one must lower and diminish oneself when in the presence of God. To this day we say "Remove your shoes!" in Hebrew when someone is being boastful or denigrating and needs a reminder that he is in the presence of someone greater and more important than the likes of him and that he should return to his natural dimensions.

In spite of all this, there are those who go barefoot not in a theatrical or qualitative way but for simple financial reasons: Abba Hilkiah, the grandson of Honi the Circle Drawer, who brought down rain, was once asked why he carries his shoes in his hands when walking but wears them when crossing areas flooded with water. His answer was this: "I see all the way, but in water I do not see." In other words, while walking I can see what might hurt the soles of my feet and so there is no need to wear out my shoes. But in water I cannot see what I am stepping on and I fear for my flesh.

As for me—since I neither grow burning bushes, nor run away from sons who rebel against me and ask for my head on a platter, nor make prophecies about political or military developments in the region, or am inclined to gimmicks to attract attention—I go barefoot for more basic reasons. First, because I can, because I have been doing it since I was born. Second, I enjoy it and this is the way I like it. I relish the direct contact of my foot on the ground and the sensation that dusty pathways and dry leaves give me, and also sandy ground and earth drenched in mud. And I am happy with the information that my foot receives from the ground and I revel in the agreeable pressure that the variable terrain applies to it. I like the game play between the muscles of the soles of my feet and toes, which do almost no work at all inside a closed shoe. Mostly, I enjoy the feeling of freedom that a bare foot gives its owner. It is no coincidence that *manoul*, the word for "lock" in Hebrew, and *naʾal*, "shoe," share the same root, whose meaning is "closure" or "imprisonment."

Even when wearing shoes, many people stumble when stepping off a sidewalk or a road onto a path or into a field, and even more when barefoot. The issue here is both habituation of the soles of the feet to unmediated contact with the terrain and also the way a person presents himself on it, and then steps onto it: the toes dig into the ground a little, gripping it, releasing, activating minor muscles, forgotten ones, recalling abilities lost to the human body a long time ago. And not only this: over time, people who go barefoot develop eyes in their heels and toes and eventually do not have to look where they are going. The foot itself sees the surface of the ground.

And sometimes, when I pause, standing barefoot on the soil without treading farther, I feel the ground holding me gently, reminding me that

even if I normally wear sandals or shoes, this is where I came from and where I belong. In short, I recommend that everyone forgo wearing shoes from time to time. Walk barefoot on the ground! It is both pleasant and beneficial to the body, reviving the spirits and offering a lesson that is undoubtedly good for the soul.

34

Figs

There are many Hebrew speakers who do not know the meaning of the word *syafot*. And many are convinced that *sitvaniyot* are just colchicums, small rosy flowers that bloom here in the autumn. But both these words signify the last figs of the season. I admit that I didn't know these important things either, until I came across them one day in the Scriptures and they filled me with great joy: first, because I enriched my vocabulary with two more beautiful, impractical words; second, because the rise and fall of vocabulary in any language of a specific field expresses the changing importance of that field in the speaker's life. This is how we deduce the importance of the fig to Hebrew speakers in the First and Second Temple, the place it occupied in their lives, and what linguistic richness developed around it. Every child knew back then that a *pagga* was an unripe fig, and a *devela* was a dried fig, the difference between a shriveled, inedible fig or *grogeret* and an overripe fig, *tsemel*, and between slices of *keziah* figs waiting to be dried, and *novelet* figs that fell from the tree. Everyone enjoyed identifying with the description of the exuberant consumption of the *bikura,* the first fig to ripen: "When he that looketh upon it seeth, while it is yet in his hand, he eateth it up."

As I related earlier, there was a large and beautiful fig tree in my garden whose trunk was punctured and eaten by longhorn beetle larvae. At first I attempted to save the tree: I inserted cotton wool soaked in gasoline into their tunnels; I cast about for them with a long piece of wire thread bent at one end like a hook, a method of destroying leopard moth larvae taught to me by my grandfather when I was a boy. I managed to catch and pull out two of them—both big and flaccid, with the hard evil head of mining machinery—but it was too late. Their brothers kept going, and the inside of the trunk was eaten away even more, until a few months later the fig tree collapsed. The disaster happened at three o'clock in the morning, and the tumult as it fell awoke me. I hastened outside and saw it lying on the ground.

I was so appalled by the murderous capabilities of these beetle larvae that for several years I avoided planting another fig tree in place of the one that died. Finally, I resolved to plant a new fig tree, in spite of all this. In selecting the seedling, I took an approach taught me by my old friend Puyu, the painter and planter: "Don't plant a fig tree in your garden if you don't know its mother."

And so, my new fig tree has an extraordinary mother whose fruits I have even tasted, and to this day the tree has never been attacked by beetle larvae. On the other hand—it did not grow. And if it grew, it did so at the rate of less than half an inch each year. I went to Puyu to ask what this meant, and he reassured me: "The tree's investing in its roots," he said, smiling broadly. But how long does it take to invest in roots? According to this rule, the roots of my fig tree have already reached China, and I still cannot sit in its shade or eat its fruit. And Puyu has meanwhile passed away, and I now have no one to ask or blame. Who knows, perhaps the tree is so busy investing in its roots that it is even ripening figs underground?

Meanwhile I buy figs in stores, receive them from friends, and, on various hikes through Israel, I pluck and eat abandoned figs. These grow in the Judean Hills and Jerusalem and the Galilean mountain range and inner lowlands. A fortunate fig tree grows out of a water hole or close to a spring and is fresh and green. A fig tree whose roots are in dry soil uncultivated by man—its leaves are wilted and slack, and the residue of its fertility is dedicated to bearing fruit. Some of these fig trees were sown by birds, and most of them are located in places that were formerly Arab villages. Like sabra hedges, unpruned olives, untrellised vines, and almonds that have become bitter—they are also witness to life here before the War of Independence.

In Hebrew, by the way, the verb *le'erot*, "to pick fruit from a fig tree," comes from the word *orr*, which means "light," because the fig tree must be visited at first light. Rising early is important; back in the days when this lovely verb was invented, there were no refrigerators, and at dawn the figs are cool and dewy and much tastier, and the wasps and flies, who are also fond of figs and who congregate around them in hot weather, are still frozen and silent.

And one more thing: if luck is with you and fennel bushes grow around the tree, a pungent, pleasant smell of anise rises up, merging with and enhancing the taste of the figs. And if nature has not provided this marriage, I recommend a pleasant alternative: chill the figs in the refrigerator, cut them in half, drizzle a little arak over their flesh, and devour.

In Proverbs it is written: "Whoso keepeth the fig tree shall eat the fruit thereof." In Hebrew the specific meaning of "keepeth" is "to watch over," in other words "to guard," but for what reason is the guarding of a simple fig tree glorified? First, because there are many who desire the fruit of the fig tree, particularly bipeds, meaning birds and humans. But guarding also connotes close supervision, including the way in which the fig ripens. As opposed to fruit trees that produce most of their crop within a short time, the fig tree produces fruit over a few weeks, extending its measured favor with wisdom: every day it honors its owners with a few new figs, and one must wake up early to pluck them before they are devoured by birds or become rotten. This makes it difficult for farmers who grow figs for marketing, but a mere person with a fig tree in his garden will be gladdened anew by the fig tree each morning.

And further ruminations arise while seeking and picking the figs: unlike the hasty picking from deciduous trees that bear fruit with pits, and the violent harvesting of olives with rakes and sticks, using the method of shaking and pulling (and in Hebrew the root of *masak*, "olive harvesting," and *mashach*, "pulling," are similar to each other), and unlike the harvesting of bunches of grapes with pruning shears, ripe figs must be surveyed and tracked and checked, not only with the eyes but also by touch—with fingers that learn the importance of gentleness and the pleasantness of erudition. When you get to a ripe, ready fruit—soft fleshed, thin cracks spreading over its skin, the gold gleaming, and the red flickering on its underside—you grasp it softly and remove it so gently that the fruit simply drops into the palm of your hand. This is because more than any other fruit tree, the fig tree is the most suggestive, the most acquiescent and alluring, and more often than not, as if asking to justify the associations with its name, the fig tree conceals its fruit within its leaves, which naturally and obviously are fig leaves, embodying everything these associations arouse.

While writing this, I recall a line from my father's poem "Figs": "Fumbling through landscape as if straining through garments toward forbidden nakedness, deep and concealed." And since figs and fingers and nakedness have already been mentioned here, I also have some advice to offer: when picked, the fig disgorges a sticky white juice from its pedicel, and it is highly recommended not to touch any delicate part of the body with fingers that have become sticky with this juice: not the eyes nor corners of the mouth or any other bodily places or tissues. By the way, folk remedies even recommend using the juice as a remedy for calluses. In other words, do not underestimate its capabilities.

In winter the fig tree is bare, but in summer it provides cool and copious shade. The harvester rests there, wolfing down figs he promised to bring back home for breakfast, and realizing a further progression of the Hebrew language. Today's bland Hebrew subtext of "peace and security" was derived from the wonderful Hebrew expression: "Every man sits under his vine and under his fig tree." And when the fig tree in question is one of the big, old abandoned fig trees I frequent, it is difficult to avoid another thought: that I, and not the person who planted the tree, now sit under it. I pick and eat its fruit. Meanwhile, under the reign of our respective thorny bushes who think themselves wise and trust in their own might, neither of us knows peace, security, or tranquility.

This is not a new phenomenon. As far back as Deuteronomy, God told the Israelites that, waiting for them in the land of Canaan, were "houses full of all good things, which thou filledst not, and wells digged, which thou diggedst not, vineyards and olive trees, which thou plantedst not." This is indeed what the Israelites found here when they conquered Canaan, and also the Philistines and Assyrians and Babylonians and Persians and Greeks and Romans and Byzantines and Crusaders and Arabs and Turks—everyone found here olives and figs they had not planted themselves, and terraces they had not built, and water holes they had not dug, and each added something of their own for the next in line. This is the story of a land promised by so many gods, a land conquered by so many conquerors, claimed by so many. And this is also the warning issued by the land to each of its children and all of its rulers.

And as for me—my fig tree still stands rebelliously and does not grow, and I do not sit in its shade or partake of its fruit. Every year it bears two early *bikura* figs, which are eaten by jaybirds before I can get to them. It seems the definition of the word *boser*, "unripe fruit," is not the same in their language as it is in mine, but perhaps a beak is less sensitive to unripe fruit than teeth and a palate. Either way, I hope that one day this fig tree will stop investing in its roots and start investing in me, too, and that it will return the love I bestow upon it. In the meantime, I continue to learn from it the importance of patience and anticipation.

35

Wasp Nest

One Sabbath, while I was eating lunch on the terrace, a wasp appeared, landing on my plate. There is nothing new about this. Wasps work on the Sabbath, too. They're attracted to meat and can smell it from afar. But this type of wasp was new to me, one I was not familiar with, bigger than the European paper wasp and smaller than the Oriental wasp, commonly known as a hornet.

Like all wasps, this one helped itself to a small portion of my meal, then took off and flew back to its nest. But the next day, as I was working in the garden, something stung my arm. It felt like a beesting, but more painful. I examined the spot, and because I was unable to see the remains of a stinger, I concluded I had been stung by a wasp.

In the past I have experienced both the mild stings of the paper wasp and the more acute ones of the hornet. This sting was harsher than the former yet weaker than the latter. I did my homework, asked around, and investigated further. I even went so far as to look for photographs and discovered that it was likely the same species that had joined me for lunch the day before, a wasp known in Israel as the German wasp. It seemed this German wasp had also done its homework, asked around, investigated further, and dug up all kinds of facts about me and my identity, because the next day I was stung for the second time. I realized that the wasp nest—the thing itself this time and not an Israeli metaphor for a terrorist cell—was right here in my garden.

I believe I have already made it clear that although I own this garden according to the rules and regulations of the State of Israel, I acknowledge the proprietary rights of the different creatures that inhabit it. But I ask them to behave in a similarly respectful way toward me, acknowledging me and my rights, particularly my statutory right to walk safely through the garden and return home in one piece. I searched for the wasp nest, and after a further infuriating sting I found it in a hole in the ground. I made a note of its location in order not to get too close, but the wasps also made a few notes of their own, and the next day I suffered another sting, this time in a different part of the garden and on a different part of my anatomy.

I discussed the situation with both myself and others. In light of the aggressiveness of these wasps and their high standards of operation, I resolved to regard myself, rather than the wasps, as a creature under threat of extinction. The battle was on.

This is the place to warn readers of a tender disposition to perhaps skip the rest of this chapter and move to the next, because from now on there will be searing descriptions of war and carnage that are not for the delicate or fainthearted. A battle against a wasp nest is a fight to the bitter end, a battle whose consequences are either to flee with no right of return or total extermination of the losing side. No consideration is given to the Geneva Conventions, no prisoners are taken, no capitulation agreements are signed, certainly not peace treaties—and the reason is simple: after a war like this, there will be no one left to sit with around the negotiating table.

From every angle, I was the underdog: one against many, my infantry against fighter airplanes; a democrat, upholder of peace, liberalism, and human rights, against a totalitarian society in which the lives of its war-riors are disposable, not to mention the lives of its enemies. But it was precisely for this reason that I knew I was going to win, because justice was on my side, and I still believe that despite the occasional success of evil, at the end of the day it is good that triumphs.

I armed myself with rags, a quarter bucket of kerosene, a two-foot stick, an alarm clock, long pants, hiking boots, a long-sleeved shirt, a headlamp, and a medium-sized rock. The reader is at leisure to imagine all kinds of war scenarios based on this list: for example, that I set the alarm clock for three in the morning, placed it by the nest, and when the wasps emerged in order to silence the annoying sound of the alarm, I approached the nest with a rag tied to the end of the stick like a flag and waved it at them as if surrendering; I blinded them with the headlamp and crushed their heads with the rock, one by one, then poured kerosene into the nest, set it alight, and rounded it all off by wearing a long-sleeved shirt in order to award myself a medal of valor.

There are other options, no less complex, depending on the extent of your imagination or craftiness, but I'll skip those scenarios and pro-ceed to a description of the actual battle as it played out: The alarm clock woke me up at one-thirty in the morning, when the wasps are inactive and gathered in their nest. I got dressed, buttoned myself up and laced myself in, strapped the headlamp to my head, dropped the rag into the bucket of kerosene, carried the bucket in my left hand and the stick and rock in my right, and went out silently into the pitch-black night. Close to destination, I switched on the headlamp and located the nest entrance.

Using the stick, I thrust the kerosene-soaked rag deep into it, placed the bucket over it—upside down, of course—put the rock over that, and beat a quick retreat home.

Despite their surprise, the wasps returned fire. It could be that my headlamp woke some of them up. I suffered four more stings in the space of ten seconds, but not even one more in the days that followed. A week later, when I removed the bucket from the nest, not so much as a single wasp surfaced. From that time forth, I have never been stung in the garden. Occasionally I come across a nest of European paper wasps in one of the bushes. I draw near, and observe. The wasps do not sting me, and I do not sting them either.

36

Lupines

A drift of blossoming lupines pleasures the eye and pleases the heart. There are plenty of places like this in Israel, and happily not all of them have been named Lupine Hill or publicized in travel supplements. It is still possible to visit them without inhaling carbon-monoxide fumes from buses, without encountering herds of ATVs, screams, shouts, bags of Doritos, toilet paper, and empty bottles of Coca-Cola.

There are lupines with white blossoms and also yellow ones, but the most common and the prettiest are blue lupines. They flower at the end of winter and spring, and their intense blue is adorned with a vertical white banner. The banner turns a reddish color after the flower has been pollinated. This is how the lupine lets insects in search of pollen know the snack bar is closed and, if you please, go to another flower. The reason is clear: It is better for both plant and insect that the insect visits only flowers with pollen and does not waste time and energy visiting flowers that have nothing to offer since they are no longer in need of pollination services.

Lupines are annuals. This means that every year new lupines sprout from last year's seeds. They grow, produce flowers and seeds—and die. Their seeds are large and tough, nestling within pods. In April and May—

depending on the temperatures and the amount of rain—the pods yellow and ripen, and when the time is right they burst open with a loud popping sound. The sides separate at the seam, curl upward all at once, and the seeds are catapulted three or even four feet away from their parents.

Lupines bloom in my garden every year. Some self-sow, but mostly I do the sowing from seeds gathered and stored after the flowering season. As I pick the pods, a pleasant crackling sound can be heard all around, and some even pop between my very fingers. I lay the entire pod in the sun, inside a large, flat plastic tub, and for a few days I listen to them, popping and jumping and generally carrying on, and I know my face is wreathed in smiles.

After the first rain, I sow the gathered seeds in a part of the garden that is saturated with sunlight, but prior to this I soak them in water for twenty-four hours. This is how I persuade them that it is a particularly rainy year and they really should sprout. I do not fling them to the ground as nature does. Instead, I make incisions in the soil at a depth of several inches with a pickax harrow, scatter the seeds, and then cover them by raking the soil. The germinating leaves soon burst forth, carried on a short stem to which are glued the seed halves, and after a few days they resemble two heartrending, dainty green hands. After that, more leaves are added, and the lupines continue to grow. It's a good idea to sow them in two cycles, spaced two to three weeks apart, in order to enjoy a double round of blossoming. You can also sow chrysanthemums and poppies between and around them; the combination of red, yellow, and blue is really very lovely.

In recent years I see more and more lupines in more and more private gardens, and sometimes even in public parks. This pleases me, of course, but I would like all gardeners who sow lupines to know that the greatest grower of lupines in the history of the Jewish people is no longer alive, nor was he actually known as a gardener—none other than Rabbi Shimon Bar Yochai.

The best-known and most meaningful connection between Bar Yochai and the plants of our land is the carob, created for him and his son above the cave in which they hid from the Romans. The carob nourished them for thirteen years. But because I am not inclined to tell tales of saints and miracles, I prefer the story of Bar Yochai and the lupines, testimony both to the wisdom of this holy man and to his practical nature. Rumor has it that even in those days, there were many ancient tombs in Tiberias, but not all were known or marked. The people of Tiberias asked him to determine the exact location of these tombs so they could build without fear of desecrating the dead. Shimon Bar Yochai, as compared with the fossilized and fearful Orthodox rabbis of today, solved the problem in an original and unexpected way. He told the people of Tiberias to sow lupines throughout the city, saying that wherever they sprouted and flourished, that would be where the tombs were. Building could be carried out anywhere the lupines did not grow.

Some claim that the lupines succeeded in growing in these areas because the dead fertilize the soil. Others claimed that they bloomed because the ground in graveyards is deep and the roots do not immediately hit a layer of rock. But lupines do not root to great depths and, if you ask my opinion, this is not a question of botany or agronomy but of common sense and basic psychology. With all due respect to desecration of the dead, Bar Yochai knew that life also has certain demands: Tiberias needed to develop, people needed homes, it was impossible to search for and clean up an entire city of bones that were hundreds of years old. This is why he came up with such a solution, which gave people something to go by, and which demonstrated Bar Yochai's knowledge of the nature of man rather than the nature of soil and plants. This is further testimony to his understanding and boldness, something that cannot be said with regard to the cowardly and lesser rabbis living in that same city today who came up with the ludicrous solution of installing pipes to drain impurities of the dead from the soil. Who would have thought such a thing possible . . . ?

As for me, I sow lupines in my garden for altogether different reasons. The issue of defilement and purity are of no particular interest to me. To be on the safe side, I never report the results of my sowing, just in case someone from the Atra Kadisha burial society shows up at my house claiming that the lupine blossoms prove there are tombs in my garden, too.

Just Like Bavaria

A few years ago someone told me about a special place here in Israel, where the cyclamen already blooms by November. He made me swear not to reveal its whereabouts, in order to avoid the immediate arrival of tens of groups of tourists, similar to those who come to see the blooming of crocuses or lupines or "carpets of anemones," as they are referred to here. I swore not to tell, took a trip there, and discovered he was right, the cyclamens there really do bloom in November, and not only that—they produce flowers before green leaves. I asked those in the know what the meaning of this behavior is and was told this is a different variety of cyclamen.

The cyclamens in my garden blossom in regular fashion: at the beginning of winter their tubers return to life and produce green foliage that begins to photosynthesize and provides nutrients to both the leaves and flowers that the plant produces some weeks later. At first I assumed they produce leaves because of the rain, sensing the moisture, but once I forgot about a few tubers I had wrapped in newspaper and put in a bucket in the larder, a place where there is neither light nor rainfall. When

I finally remembered them, I discovered they were trying to produce leaves. They were doing it, I surmised, because they sensed the drop in temperature.

Either way, time passed, and a few years later a number of cyclamen plants flowered in November, and they did so before producing leaves. Had a different variety sprung up in my garden, too? Perhaps it was simple jealousy, an attempt to recapture my heart and curtail my visits to those special cyclamens? While I was still wondering about all this, the anemones bloomed early as well, and that same year they were in flower by December.

Again, I do not remember the exact year it happened, but I do remember that the pattern of rain that year was a little problematic. Winter began early, with a particularly cold and rainy week, and immediately afterward there was a long dry spell. I suppose the rain and the cold roused my cyclamens, but the aridity and heat that followed prompted them to bring forth flowers before leaves, because at such difficult hours they preferred to be fruitful and multiply for the next generation, and only later worried about themselves and their own nutrition by producing green leaves to photosynthesize.

The words "preferred" and "worried" may be misleading. Is it possible that my cyclamen plants are able to think and make calculations? That they remember, learn from experience, and make plans? Did they show motherly altruism here, deciding to starve themselves for the good of future generations? And perhaps evolution forged within them a few operational programs that were awaiting realization according to external conditions?

Since I am no scientist, I allow myself to hypothesize not just hypotheses but feelings. Mostly the feeling of anxiety that fills the bulbs and tubers, and—even more than that—the seeds. Geophytes—plants possessing bulbs and tubers—have independent food-storage organs available in times of need, but the seed concealed beneath the soil waiting for rain is equipped with energy supplies purely for the germination and growth of a small root and a few leaflets, and from this time forth it must make do with sunlight, rainwater, and the goodness of the soil. It must proceed cautiously because the moment sprouting occurs, there is no opportunity to stop, let alone go backward. If it sprouts in November and rain fails to fall in December, there is a chance it might die. Then what will it do? I can almost hear the anxious conversations taking place underground: To sprout? Now? Did anyone catch the weather forecast? Is it worth waiting for more rain? Or maybe next year?

In more difficult areas, such as the desert, there are seeds that can wait years in dry ground until a wet and rainy season persuades them to sprout. And then they rise up in their multitudes and flower, bestowing upon us the rare and wonderful sight of hills covered with grass and a bounteous and astonishing desert in bloom. This was the case in the winter of 2014–15 when the Judean Desert and Negev riverbeds were enveloped in green and purple, pink and white, yellow and red. The same happened in the winter of 1991–92, and I recall taking a German poet, who was visiting Israel, for a quick trip to the Judean Desert. Mutual friends asked me to do this on the assumption that the desert landscape would be a new and unique experience for our German visitor.

As I mentioned, this was a particularly rainy winter, and the desert was enjoying it, too. Water flowed through the ravines, and the arid landscape was entirely green. Dense grass and plentiful flowers covered the hills. The German poet, a hefty, likable guy, sat next to me in the car. He seemed rather bored. "Wilhelm," I told him, "you need to understand we're in the desert, where it's usually arid and everything is brown and yellow. You're lucky to see a miracle that only happens once in decades."

The poet smiled at me convivially, scanned the landscape tiredly, and said, "Just like Bavaria."

I was not insulted. "Yes," I said, "just like Bavaria," and decided to forgo an explanation on seeds, bulbs, and precipitation in the Middle East. But I returned from this with an unexpected gain: the expression "just like Bavaria" joined my dictionary of expressions, and I use it often. Whenever someone promises I will see something extraordinary, or gives me a taste of some particularly delectable delicacy, or takes me to an outstanding exhibition or a place with an exceptional view, and the reality does not match expectations that were aroused by the promise—I taste, I look, I sniff around, I exclaim, "Just like Bavaria," and when they wonder what on earth I mean, I say I am merely quoting from a German poem.

38

Procrastination and Ridicule

Among the many complaints, rebukes, and accusations I have heard over the last years concerning my opinions and behavior, my personality, and the bitter fate I impose upon the characters in my books, there are some that relate to my garden. First, about its shape: my garden is neither neatly organized nor well kept and, as I have already divulged, is dry for many days of the year. Second, the essence of my employment there is regarded by those who claim to have my best interests at heart as nothing but a distraction from my real work. I have even heard them use the word "procrastinator"—meaning that in their opinion the garden provides me with reasons to delay the really important tasks and to waste time on what they define as nonsense.

In my defense, I must say that there are seasons in which the gardener must drop everything and go out to his garden, even if he is in charge of an emergency room or happens to be the prime minister and definitely if he is a mere writer of tales. When the poppy capsules turn yellow, the protagonists of my stories can wait. The seeds must be gathered before they fall. And when weeds blossom, they must be cut or pulled out before they have time to produce unwanted seeds that will sprout next year. I am punctilious in this regard, but privately I admit that, here and there, I see justification in what the slanderers and ridiculers say, because I often get up from my desk for gardening jobs that are not so very urgent.

For example, I might suddenly feel the need to check whether the small-flowered pancratium has begun blooming. At first I repress the impulse, but it quickly becomes so bothersome that I realize if I don't go out into the garden to inspect it, I won't be able to concentrate on my writing. This is why—out of concern for my work—I go out to these flowers, but on the way I notice a few weeds that need pulling, and as I stoop over them, I see a tiny hyacinth squill that has sprouted prematurely, because a nearby irrigation pipe turned its world upside down and confused it. Since it is not supposed to be there, I go to my toolbox to fetch a spade, see the power scythe next to it, remember that I need to buy a wire cutter, and drive off to the store. I admit: things like this have happened more than once.

Another claim of those who have appointed themselves my educators, foremen, or even my guardians is that I have become ridiculous, pathetic even, when I describe the garden and narrate what goes on there, writing about it as I do now, for example, or showing it, or—worse still—displaying photos of it to people who have no interest in the flowering times of crocuses and the best way to store poppy seeds; nor any interest in my musings about the importance of identifying plants and a knowledge of nature in general, the connection to our homeland, the beauty of the gladioli, the wisdom of the squills, and so forth.

I have already witnessed a few impersonations of myself that were actually quite good, crawling on all fours, sniffing the air, saying "Agrostemma" six times in one sentence, skipping between the hyssop and savory when the morning zephyr blows through the monocotyledon dress I wove myself on an organic loom, like Mrs. Leo Hunter in Dickens's *Posthumous Papers of the Pickwick Club*, who gets dressed in the costume of Minerva and recites her own "Ode to an Expiring Frog."

But all this ridicule only arouses compassion within me. I hear and see those stiff-necked types and know that it is only jealousy and self-righteousness speaking from their throats while I adhere to my beliefs. So let them go their way and I'll go mine.

And what exactly is this way? Well now, Hillel the Elder described these feelings in words more beautiful than I am capable of, expressing them more succinctly than I could ever hope to do: "To the place that my heart loves, there my feet lead me." Regretfully, I dare not apply this to everything, nor am I able to do so, but I always let my feet lead me to my beloved garden, even if sometimes I appear ridiculous, even very ridiculous.

Fortunately, I am the only one to witness my greatest moments of embarrassment and ludicrousness. For example, once I found myself at ten o'clock in the morning lying under my desk instead of sitting at it. To be more precise: lying on my stomach, one hand groping in the dark under the drawers. What was I looking for there? Not an important note that had fallen, or a beloved pen that had rolled under the desk, but two brownish-purple cyclamen seeds, each less than a tenth of an inch in size.

How did these two seeds get under my table? That morning I moved some cyclamen seeds that had been drying in a bowl to a jar where they would await planting, and two of them fell to the floor and rolled under the table. From every logical angle, horticultural or financial, I shouldn't have done anything at all. I already had plenty of seeds from that year; in my plant trays, hundreds of baby cyclamens were growing from last year's seeds; and in the garden itself, hundreds of mature cyclamens resided, grown from seeds planted over the years. In other words, I could certainly handle the loss of two seeds. The true gardener, however, is not measured by economic calculations but by his devotion to and love for his protégées.

Consequently, I quickly lie down under the table in order to look for the lost seeds.

To be more precise: At first I got up from my chair and stooped over the approximate spot where the seeds had fallen—and saw nothing. Then I got down on my knees and peeked under the table—not a thing. I lay on my stomach—still nothing. I reached out with one hand and groped about in the darkness—*gurnisht*. I lay there, and while part of my brain processed the subtable information that the tips of my fingers transmitted to me, a different part of the brain busied itself with this question: Had I completely lost my mind?

I admitted then and I admit now, I had no answer to this question. Those good souls I mentioned earlier certainly had the answers, and they told me so on sundry occasions. I was well aware of the ridicule that such situations aroused, but I knew exactly why I was lying on the floor looking for two cyclamen seeds under the table: not because I would miss them, but because they were in distress. I was not the only one—at this point, the seeds also understood that they had fallen not to the ground but to a hard floor, not under a radiant sun or a sky that gathers rain clouds, but under a table and a ceiling.

I imagined how bad they felt with the knowledge that their fate was sealed. They would be unable to sprout, put down roots, grow and blossom, or raise a new generation of cyclamens. A person must be heartless not to help seeds in such distress, all the more if he grows cyclamens, and the seeds are those he gathered in order to sow and grow in his own garden.

*I*n several of my books, I attempted to describe human emotion: love and revenge, anger and longing, hatred, disappointment, yearning and mourning, satisfaction, lust, grief and happiness. Except that all this

failed to prepare me for describing in words the emotions of a cyclamen seed experiencing such disaster. With regard to my own emotions on this point—this lying-down point, to be precise—I can testify to feelings of compassion and guilt, and a wish to lend a hand. I therefore got up off the floor and opened the drawer where my trusty headlamp should have been, but as usual it was not there. I searched until I found it on one of the shelves in the library, I flicked the switch—and nothing happened.

For a moment, I entertained the possibility of going to the corner store in the nearby village to buy new batteries for the flashlight, but the voice of reason prevailed. I decided I had done more than enough, and that there was a limit to the effort a person should make in such a situation, even if he grows and loves wildflowers, particularly cyclamens. The two seeds could go to hell and I would go back to my work. This is exactly what I did: I went back to my chair, sat down, stared hard at the computer screen, drew my fingers close to the keyboard, and a quarter of an hour later realized that as long as those two seeds were crying out for my help under the table—I would get no work done.

Fortunately, I remembered the headlamp in my car that I use on hikes. I fetched it, strapped it to my forehead, reverted to my previous position on the floor, and switched it on. I could not see the seeds, but while lying there I certainly saw myself and realized there are situations in which it is better for a person to be alone, particularly if someone else might see him. But because I was already lying there, and the headlamp was working, and in any event I already knew that I was out of line, I searched and groped and shone the light until I found those two seeds and returned them to their friends in the jar, and I was happy. Perhaps even happier than the seeds themselves.

Since I'm in a confessional mood, I will reveal another secret: when no one is listening, I am in the habit of simulating, in a loud voice, mono-logues and dialogues of animals, plants, and even inanimate objects—like conversations between socks that have returned from trips abroad with socks that were left behind in the drawer, or the cries of a cucumber when I peel it with a sharp knife.

Now, in the precise voice of a cyclamen seed and with a perfect imitation of its accent, I said, "Where were you? We were worried about you . . ." and "We thought we'd never see you again . . . ," and I answered, "Nah, we went exploring, because later we're going to put down roots and it'll be too late . . ." and I decided that perhaps I am not as crazy as some people, myself included, think I am.

An idea then popped into my head that I should keep the two seeds apart from the others and that I should plant them in their own pot, so that I would know that these were the two cyclamens I found and saved the day they fell under my writing desk. For a moment I considered hitting myself over the head for my own foolishness, but I calmed down, because it was as clear to me as three times three that a few years from now, when I go outside to see the cyclamens I sowed this year blooming in the garden, those two will say to me, "Thank you," and I will hear them, I will know it is them, and I will answer, "It was my pleasure."

39

The Stupid Woodpecker

Village is not the tranquil, quiet place it's supposed to be. It is true there are no buses on the streets, no honking of car horns, no ambulance sirens or police vehicles, and there are far fewer shouts and cries, but the air force takes off and lands at a nearby base, and at night dogs bark, and on Sabbath mornings we sometimes get a beastly bunch of flying drones that hang low, gliding slowly above our heads and making an awful racket.

Nature's creatures also make a lot of noise, especially birds: jaybirds that gather in the branches of the pecan tree for karaoke parties and contests of cursing and castigation, and parakeets who argue with the entire world. Once a woodpecker threatened to drive me insane, pecking away for three solid days, drumming with its beak and aggravating me endlessly.

I usually enjoy these pecking barrages as they switch between automatic and single shots, and I love watching and listening to the woodpecker as it busies itself. I watch the woodpecker until it becomes aware of my gaze, releases a cry of alarm, and flees by swooping up and down, leading enemies and other raptors astray. It is quick to disappear into the foliage of another tree, out of which the sound of pecking soon recurs.

But the woodpecker I have in mind was not looking for food or pecking at a tree but rather at a nesting box I had put there for titmice. The woodpecker pecked away and did not stop even when I glared at him with a particularly menacing look in my eyes. This time, in spite of the unwritten agreement I have with all the creatures in my garden, that they refrain from harassing me and I refrain from disturbing them, I finally marched out of the house and shooed the woodpecker away. I shooed it away, and it came back. I shooed it away yet again, but the woodpecker kept going—returning to the nesting box, pecking away incessantly.

The woodpecker's persistence arose out of its desire to nest in that very nesting box. But the entrance to the box was designed for titmice and was thus too small for the woodpecker. This is why it busied itself with what woodpeckers know best: widening the opening to the nesting box. The problem was that a flat metal ring had been affixed to the opening in order to prevent precisely this, a ring that even the woodpecker's robust beak could not shatter.

The titmouse, for whom the nesting box was intended, is a small and pretty songbird with a pale yellow chest and a thin black line from neck to underbelly. In Hebrew the titmouse is known as *yargazi,* implying anger, yet in spite of such a name this bird is one of the nicer occupants of my garden. The male titmouse is a gifted singer, and his loud, beautiful singing announces that my garden, in fact, belongs to him. This announcement is not intended for my ears, but those of other male titmice. Like most males, they are so gifted that they want to bestow upon the world offspring in their own image. This is why they need both territory and a mate, and they are prepared to defend both with all their might and to sing about it at the top of their voices.

The titmice build their nests in cavities with narrow entrances. If a person attaches to a tree a nesting box that meets all their requirements, it is highly likely the titmice will nest there. This is why, one day, I went

off to meet a person by the name of Shai HaLevy from Moshav Ram-On, who builds nesting boxes for birds, and I returned home with one of those boxes. I attached it to the trunk of the terebinth tree that stands close to my house, at the exact height and in the direction that I had been told—in other words, not directly facing the ravages of rain and wind, but in the opposite direction, and in a place where I could watch the nesting box through the window.

Less than two days later, a pair of titmice began entering and exiting the box, bearing nesting materials. I waited a few more days, until I could no longer restrain myself. I climbed up a ladder, opened the lid to the box—Shai had installed hinges on it—peeped inside, and discovered a nest with six eggs in it. The two parents promptly arrived back at the nest carrying insects in their beaks. I came back to take another look inside, and six ravenous yellow beaks gaped up at me hungrily. I continued following their progress with interest and enjoyment until they flew the nest. To my joy, their parents were quick to build a new nest in the box, raising another generation of offspring.

As for the woodpecker, it continued pecking away, unimpressed by my success in the titmouse-raising academy, and perhaps even envious of the nesting box I had given them. This was the situation: the woodpecker pecked and pecked, the ring did not yield, I went out and shooed it away, the woodpecker flew off only to return to peck some more, the ring held up, I shooed the woodpecker away, and the stubborn idiot refused to concede. It returned, gripping the nesting box of the titmice and striking the metal ring with its indefatigable beak, but the ring was also indefatigable and held its own. When evolution created a head for the woodpecker with sophisticated shock absorbers and a beak capable of penetrating, widening, and digging, it apparently forgot that a head also contains a brain. The woodpecker's brain, more's the pity, never really developed. Nor did that same evolution do anything to bolster the woodpecker's ability to assess or improvise.

If only that noisy idiot woodpecker had pecked around the ring rather than directly at the ring itself, it would have done away with the obstacle in a matter of moments, but the woodpecker knows only one thing—how to widen the perimeter of an opening. Even if that opening is made of metal, this is what the woodpecker aims for. Who knows? Perhaps the ceaseless hammerings it hammers into the trees may nevertheless make their mark on the woodpecker's brain. Let us not forget from the start that we are talking about a creature who is, literally, a birdbrain.

40

The Locked Garden

Hikes I have hiked around the world have given me the opportunity to visit gardens and parks both sleek and stylish, wild and dilapidated. I generally prefer gardens that have not been tweezer weeded, where plants are not arranged in trios or pruned into footballs, columns, or—even worse—into all kinds of animal shapes and forms. But of all the parks I ever visited, the two that affected me most deeply and which will be forever engraved upon my memory are both immaculately kept gardens. Both are in Israel, and both influenced me in a positive way, each one in its own time and place.

The two I am talking about are the gardens of the Jewish Institute for the Blind in Jerusalem and the Bahá'í Gardens north of Acre. I visited the former many times as a boy and the latter several times as a young man. Since those days, I have visited neither. I will further add that I experienced both gardens with a different sense of sight and under circumstances that do not typify a regular visit to a garden. I saw the gardens at the Jewish Institute for the Blind through the eyes of a small boy, eyes that perceived and remembered differently from the eyes of my adult self today. I saw the Baháʼí Gardens near Acre only in darkness, and both these gardens I visited clandestinely.

The garden of the Jewish Institute for the Blind was the forbidden and longed-for garden of my childhood days. Back then we lived in the Kiryat Moshe housing project in Jerusalem and, as I already mentioned, we moved there close to the end of its construction. Small gardens began to color the housing project, a little here and a little there, but the trees had yet to grow tall or spread their branches, nor did they provide shade for the bare concrete sidewalk. On the other hand, the garden across the street that belonged to the Jewish Institute for the Blind boasted trees and large bushes, cool shady corners and flowers that offered agreeable fragrances. It also contained two lawns. More than once we played games you wouldn't believe possible with the blind children on the front lawn—chase, dodgeball, and even hide-and-seek. But the back lawn, the more concealed one, was forbidden territory, and the wielder of its flaming sword, which turned in every direction, was the guard, a herculean amputee who moved with incredible speed in a wheelchair he commandeered by accelerating on two handles with his colossal hands.

There, in the forbidden section of the garden, were gravel paths lined with lilies and clipped hedgerows of privet and thuja, and a small pond in which large indolent goldfish practiced barrel rolls and swam around. There was a lawn with wooden and stone benches set down at its edges. The entire area, I guess, could not have been larger than a quarter of an acre, but back then it appeared to be the size of a royal garden, albeit more beautiful than any of the royal gardens of Paris, Madrid, London, or Kyoto, which I visited years later.

We usually entered the garden of the Institute for the Blind through the iron gate at the back, a gate that was always locked and bolted with a lock and heavy chain. We climbed stealthily up on one side of the gate, sometimes in a gang and sometimes alone, and equally stealthily climbed down the other side. I entered the boundaries of the garden and immediately sank down into the sweet depths of stolen water. This feeling, however, was coupled with one of dread. Not just because of the horror stories we had heard about the guard's bad temper but also because of the aura of strangeness and mystery, and the murky atmosphere I imagine was generated by the blind children's eyes as they fumbled their way through foliage or learned the names of flowers according to touch and smell. Since then, as I said, I have not returned to this garden. But eventually I wrote about it in *His House in the Desert,* describing it this same way, without actually going there to see if it still exists and without comparing it with the special picture I have of it in my memory.

The Baháʼí Gardens near Acre—for the Baháʼís, by the way, this site is more important than its better-known and bigger brother in Haifa—I got to know some years later, when I was a new recruit in the Israeli army. The army base for new recruits of the Golani Brigade I served in was located opposite Bustan HaGallil. The Baháʼí Gardens, whose existence I was unaware of, were close by.

Boot camp was not physically difficult for me. While studying at high school I took numerous long hikes on foot, and every summer I worked hard at my uncles' place in Nahalal. Mentally, it was another story, because in the boot-camp base of Golani in 1966, a certain atmosphere prevailed, and there were people the likes of whom I had never met in my entire life. I remember when we first arrived there, before we even had time to alight from the truck, there was a terrible yelling, and in front of our eyes a fleeing officer appeared, hotly pursued by a recruit waving a metal angle bar and trying to hit the officer. While we were still getting ready for our first roll call, one of the recruits approached me and showed me a close-up pornographic photograph of a man and a woman. I could not see their faces, but other parts of their anatomies clarified for me the fact that there were things in the world I had not even thought about, let alone done.

"Do you wanna buy it?" he asked.

I must have hesitated for a moment, because the guy added, with a note of solicitation, "It's my girlfriend with my brother."

In the days that followed I discovered squad commanders and sergeants, most of whom were generally lowbrow but extremely creative in the field of bullying, boring monotonous training exercises, and drills that drove me out of my mind.

One night, after completing guard duty and awakening the next soldier in rotation, I did not go back to sleep but found myself walking along the perimeter of the base searching for a breach in the fence, rumors of which had spread through the camp. I found it, crawled through to the other side, stood up, and walked off, soon arriving at a high wall. I climbed the wall and saw beyond it a garden that stretched out and whose beauty was evident, even under cover of night. I lowered myself into the garden and strolled through it.

In a filthy uniform, my body drenched in sweat, I felt like a pauper in a palace or a trespasser at the Holy of Holies, but also like a visitor to Wonderland. The garden was beautifully designed, a garden that exuded culture. Luminescent paths shone in the darkness, and cypresses stood erect as spears. The trees and shrubs were so meticulously pruned that our sergeant major, whose sole gardening ambitions boiled down to the whitewashing of tree trunks, could not even begin to imagine something like this.

Every garden planted and cared for by man presents a stylized struggle between nature and culture. The garden I have today, for example, looks to some people like a plot of land that belongs to no one, but those in the know immediately discern the signs of human toil and predilection. The Bahá'í Gardens revealed to me that night were at the other end of the gardening spectrum: meticulously designed and better maintained than any garden I have ever known. Whoever planned and planted it made use of the plants' natural features. However, they channeled the expression of these natural features in a way that does not exist in nature but was rather made to conform to their own values.

As a person who neither belongs to the Bahá'í community nor understands its principles of faith, this garden reminded me that outside boot camp, yet so close to it, existed a civilization with aesthetic values. It also reminded me that I belong to the family of man and am no stray dog, that I am a person of culture rather than a beast of burden. I walked along the garden paths at length, until the edges of the eastern horizon turned pink, at which point I hurriedly returned to the wall, the breach in the fence, the army base.

I snuck back there on a number of occasions, always after guard duty in the wee hours of the morning. Each time, the place filled me with renewed energy, hope, and the knowledge I could always return to human culture. It reminded me that beyond the foolish drills we were obliged to practice, the imbecilic roars we were obliged to roar, the jogging around the base with beds on our backs, and all the other instructive and formative activities, a benevolent garden awaited me.

From a certain point of view this garden was witness to a different way of life, a wider and larger and more demanding discipline than that demanded of us at boot camp. From other perspectives, both places had the same intentions despite their differences: to present to those entering their gates alternative atmospheres and values and a desire to change and renew—but one was through coercion and taming and arbitrariness, and the other was through expansion of the soul and the heart and the lungs.

I am not feigning innocence here. I am reluctantly aware that human societies require not only gardens but also military bases, yet I try to remember who serves whom and where my priorities should lie.

Sometimes, on my way up north, I travel on the Acre–Rosh Hanikra highway, and my eyes always wander to the east as if of their own accord, seeing and remembering. The boot camp no longer exists, but the garden is still there, and I have not forgotten my nighttime visits. As I said, I have not entered that garden since then, with or without permission, under cover of night or in broad daylight, but on every journey to the area I give thanks from the bottom of my heart to the Bahá'í gardeners who planted and cultivated it.

41

Compost in the Composter

A mong the special creatures in my garden is a composter, but before I explain why I define it as a creature, I must apologize for not using the Hebrew name given to it by the Academy of the Hebrew Language—*madshen*—nor do I use the Hebrew name given by the Academy of the Hebrew Language for the compost it produces: *d'shonet*. Both these innovations were coined in Hebrew from the root *dashan,* which in biblical Hebrew describes something plump and healthy but also denotes the sacrificial ashes in the temple.

I renounce these two names in Hebrew. It is true that words like "compost" and "composter" are indeed borrowed from foreign languages, but they have all become part of our standard vocabulary, just like "telephone," "radio," "sandal," "academy," "bravo," "*ciao ciao,*" and "*yallah* bye." But there is an even more important reason—in both these words, *d'shonet* and *madshen,* the *sh* follows *d,* a hard consonant. This makes pronunciation difficult, and whoever invented words with such phonetic land mines must also have equipped them with a self-destructive mechanism.

Despite all this, we have learned a useful lesson: usually it is easy to speak the words and more difficult to actually do them, but here the tables are turned—it is much easier to make compost in a composter than to say *d'shonet* and *madshen.* How nice it would be if this were true in other spheres of our lives.

But the real topic here is the composter itself. Like many others, I also recycle various kinds of waste. I have always been punctilious about throwing empty bottles, used batteries, cartons, bad books, and old newspapers into the appropriate recycling bin. But from the day the composter arrived in my garden I discovered it is far loftier than all that revolting recycling, a magical device. You throw garbage into it from your desk and sink and refrigerator and larder, and after a few months of hocus-pocus it gives you fragrant compost with which to fertilize your garden. All this happens without your having to do any work—just a quick stir from time to time—without electricity, gasoline, machinery, air pollutants, or wasted resources. Definitely the miracle of the trash can.

I well remember the day the composter arrived at my garden. I placed it not too near yet not too far away from the house, and that very day I began throwing my organic waste into its jaws. An important change occurred immediately, not to the composter, nor the garden, but to the trash can at home, which overnight became dry, lightweight, and never smelled bad again.

After a few weeks I became convinced that my new vocation contradicted one of the most important laws of physics, none other than the conservation of mass. The simplest of observations reveals that all waste goes into the composter, yet the composter is never full. Sometimes its content even decreases without anything having been removed from it. There's a scientific explanation to this: the organic substances in the composter break down, decreasing in volume and weight. But in the context of our relationship, I prefer to treat it as just another alluring characteristic shrouded in mystery.

Indeed, the composter is a very special contraption. In its initial days at my house I already felt that throwing organic waste into it was an unsatisfactory description, too simplified to describe my relationship with it and the influence it has on me. Since I felt I did not know enough and perhaps was even making the mistakes of a novice, I began to take more of an interest in the composter, researching and investigating. I asked, read, learned, and even hooked up with other composterists. We chatted about what was happening in the depths of our composters—conversations about the good fresh smell that the composter gives off when the compost is ready. These conversations are reminiscent of conversations between young parents on burping and various other productions of their little darlings.

Gradually it dawned on me that I had entered a whole new world in which new people lived. I do not know if this is characteristic of composterists or gardeners, or characteristic of Jews in general, or all of these banded together, but within a short while I realized that in this sphere of interest there are also believers and nonbelievers, extremists and moderates, reform and Orthodox, Lithuanians and Hasidim, Admurs and their worshippers, mystics, literal interpreters, and allegorists.

I'll try to explain the complexity of this by using a familiar example: Just as we all celebrate Seder night at Pesach, all composterists throw leftovers into their composters. But just as we celebrate Pesach according to various strange and different traditions, what is customary in one ethnic group is not only uncustomary but forbidden in the other. There are different traditions, different melodies, recipes, different laws of leavening, differences of opinion and styles, as accepted within our nation—these differences arouse levels of scorn for others, loathing, compassion, and most of all doubts about the way they live.

There are light composterers—like me, for example—who withhold meat and fish leftovers from the composter. I do this not for ideological reasons but to prevent dogs, cats, and jackals from attempting to break into it. But the compost fanatics put all organic material into their composter, including meat, and the most fervent among them include even animal poop, and as is customary in our parts, here, too, there is a polemic to be polemicized: Is it every piece of animal poop or only the dung of grass eaters? Not to mention the radicals, who throw their own poop into the composter.

Once, I was even invited to a meeting of such fundamentalists, but, for obvious reasons, I decided to keep my distance. Oh my soul, come not thou into their secret! And unto their excrement mine honor, be not thou united. I set myself a logical and hygienic limit, that my composter and I would handle anything that had not passed through the digestive system of developed creatures—leftovers from preparation of meals and the meals themselves, plate refugees and waste from cooking pots that does not include, as I said before, scraps of meat or fish.

Incidentally, the professionals house special worms in their composters to break down waste, and there are others like me who rely on the Lord God above to invite insects to lay eggs from which maggots will hatch, attracting all kinds of vermin and bugs, and all these gluttons will do the job. A composter like this needs a connection to the earth—a characteristic I admire in people, too—and so when I peek into my composter, and mostly when I stir the contents with a pitchfork, I discover that all kinds of creatures of the verminous kind, the crawling, the swarming, the creeping, are those who really enjoy the banquet I have prepared for them. And I am not alarmed by the cloud of flies that rises up in front of me when I open the lid, *au contraire*! It is a sign that my composter is working.

In its own quiet way, the composter has a good influence not only on its contents but also on its owner. Beyond the pleasant sense of belonging to nature's cycles and ways, it causes irregularities and exceptions unconnected to fanaticism, harmless ones that are even amusing both to the person involved and those who are with him. One of my friends, who naturally requested anonymity, makes a habit of dropping in on neighbors and friends who do not own composters, bucket in hand, begging for scraps. His composter, he says, is "hungry." As for me—I have caught myself actually withholding food from my own mouth on a number of occasions, leaving a tithe of bread and salad on the plate so that my composter will have something to munch on.

And as I said earlier, the composter possesses additional attributes of a living creature which further endear it to the heart: it heats up and cools down, needs oxygen and sometimes a little water as well, its innards shift and churn, it has a metabolism and also a relationship with its owner and the surrounding environment. To my mind, it also has senses and consciousness, and this is why I relate to the composter not simply as an important ecological garden appliance but as a pet and even a friend.

Sometimes, when I walk past the composter, I see it watching me and I smile back. Sometimes I go up to it, open the lid just to peek in, as if asking what's up and how's it going. This is further reason for me to continue saying and writing "compost" and "composter," because if I say *d'shonet* and *madshen* the composter might not know I am addressing it—and will therefore be insulted.

And I have one more thing to say in praise of the composter. In its own modest way, the composter is thought provoking. How come in other spheres of life, when we put all kinds of garbage, waste matter, dirt, and filth in one place, we are still surrounded by all kinds of garbage, waste matter, dirt, and filth, while the composter turns it all into useful material that is fragrant and agreeable, fertile and fertilizing. What a pity it cannot open its mouth and teach us its secrets.

42

Spiders and Snakes

There are numerous spiders in my garden, and there are also a few representatives in my house: long-legged ones that spin their webs in corners of the ceiling, short-legged ones that do not spin webs but rather stroll across the wall and leap upon their prey like miniature leopards; and sometimes lovely radial webs are constructed between the posts of the balcony railings, and when I notice a web like this I make a point of watching its owner weaving it anew by night.

I neither remove nor drive away any of them, despite the fact that I was once bitten by a house spider known as the brown recluse. Its bite can cause localized gangrene and may require surgery. This same recluse spider hid inside a shirt I was wearing, and I was lucky enough to feel its presence immediately. I struck it without actually seeing it when the spider was on the inside of my shirt. Its bite was weaker than it could have been, and the results were similarly less severe.

From time to time a scary-looking spider appears. It is large, black, and hairy, and it goes by the name of the black furrier and belongs to the tarantula family. Its bite is not dangerous but can be painful. Although I am not black, do not bite, and am not hairy, I am bigger and stronger than the black furrier, and apparently more intelligent. For this reason, when I see one in the garden, I leave it alone, but when I see one in the house I place a sheet of paper on the floor in front of the spider—it lifts up a pair of front legs and waves them threateningly—and I push it with a light touch from behind. The spider immediately moves onto the sheet of paper, displaying surprise and insult. I carry the sheet of paper outside and sweep the spider off it onto the garden soil, where it is free to live. Because there, in the garden, live the truly serious spiders: wolf spiders, orb weavers, grass spiders, and, one day, I even saw a black widow spider.

The orb weaver is the biggest weaver of webs that I know. Its web is so strong that a person coming across it while walking in a field will feel the resistance of its threads. As a boy, I saw and felt those webs many times, both in the fields of Nahalal, especially between rows of vine, and also in the field close to the neighborhood where I lived in Jerusalem. Today I no longer see it. A few years ago, an orb weaver spun a large web close to the entrance to the house, and I rejoiced with great joy and watched it for several hours. But summer passed and the orb weaver, in a spidery kind of way, disappeared with it, and the next summer there were no rightful heirs to take its place.

Within the rosemary and lavender bushes reside tiny spiders who spin webs that resemble hammocks, and large grass spiders, too. Their webs are thick and dense and are gathered into a deep funnel within which they hide. When an insect is caught in the web and tries to extricate itself, the spiders sense its palpitations, pounce on it immediately, and drag it back into the funnel.

Wolf spiders are similarly large and live in shafts in the soil. I have never caught them digging these shafts, and it is certainly possible that they simply take over and improve existing holes, but they certainly invest much work and planning in their building. They cover the sides of the opening and the walls of the shaft with a fine, dense sheet of webbing to ease climbing and prevent collapse, particularly needed when pouncing out of the lair to chase prey.

And there is another spider I enjoy looking at. It lives right inside flowers, a logical place from which to ambush insects. Its shape resembles that of a crab and its coloration changes like that of a chameleon: the spider turns white when among virgin's bower or squill, and reddish on Chinese honeysuckle. It typically creeps up on its prey or stands and waits, motionless, legs akimbo. The insect, wallowing inside the flower and gorging itself on pollen and nectar, does not notice the gradual tightening of the spider's legs around it until it is too late. Because of its resemblance to a tiny crab and also because of its hunting ground, this lovely spider is known as the flower crab spider.

There is only one genuinely dangerous spider in my garden, the black widow I previously mentioned. In contrast to the furrier spider, whose shape is scary and mannerisms threatening, the black widow spider is small, comely, and delicate. Sometimes it is adorned with red markings, but its bites can be deadly. One day I came across a widow spider in my garden. I placed it in a jar, brought the jar inside, and began deliberating: Should I keep the spider or give it to someone else? And if the latter, should I let the designated victim know of this gift he or she is about to receive? Or should I just wait to read the bereavement notices in the newspaper? And most important: To whom should I give it? And why? Might this be a personal vendetta or a public service for one and all?

All kinds of candidates immediately came to mind for all sorts of reasons. Finally, I kept the widow in my own garden, because—if it is to be a wild one—let there be danger, too. Since then I have not seen it. Perhaps the spider died in winter the way spiders do, but I reckon it produced offspring, and I even wonder if some of them are still in my garden. I say this because some of those who visit the garden—uninvited guests, pooping dogs, brides being photographed, tax collectors, and thieves—will think twice before visiting. Aside from that, like those who hang BEWARE OF BITING DOG signs on their gates, I hereby announce there may be black widow spiders in my garden. With this announcement I declare myself exempt from any complaint or legal action.

Venomous centipedes, black scorpions, and snakes also appear in the garden. Sometimes a whip snake appears, an amiable and elegant creature that is harmless but whose numbers are dwindling because it, too, is targeted by the feline population. Occasionally I come across a coin-marked snake—a semivenomous snake—between tree branches, when the birds whose nest the snake is climbing to gather around it and kick up a god-awful commotion. But I have also seen a viper in my garden on a few occasions, and when it happens I spring into action and capture the snake alive using a mop and a stick. I hold it for a while—one hand on its neck and the other on its tail—and after my heartbeat returns to normal and my legs feel less like calf's-foot jelly, I carry it to the forest and set it free.

Why do I play this dangerous game? First of all, because I can. To be more precise—because I still can. Second, because very few games remain that can be played without being persecuted for desecrating the name of the Lord, desecrating politeness, political correctness, and various other crimes and sins. I also do it in order to keep fit and to generate a bit of adrenaline, a substance that does good things to a person. And also, I admit, to strengthen my standing among members of the collective agricultural movement of the Jezreel Valley, who are way more manly and robust than I, and the majority of whom can carry a bull on their shoulders, but who are terrified of vipers. I do this for a further reason, because there is also a wild garden in the heart of man and it, too, is of importance and has rights. More precisely, not quite in the heart, but under the diaphragm, in a wonderful place, a decent and honest one, where intuition flourishes and butterflies flutter, otherwise known as butterflies in the stomach.

Aside from that, the day will come for me to stop. A person must know his limitations and recognize the decline of his abilities with time, and just as I stopped riding a motorcycle, the day will come when I will stop writing books and trapping vipers. For example—in my adolescence I would trap and free snakes, but I stopped because I realized I no longer had the dexterity or the accuracy, and I began to feel fear. The black whip snake is faster, stronger, and more aggressive than the viper. It is not venomous but is difficult to catch alive, and its bite can wound and cause pain.

Once or twice each summer a whip snake passes through my garden,

and for the last few years, rather than chasing after it, I simply observe. I enjoy the fortitude and elegance that radiates from its body. But one day I found a large black snake inside my composter. I was about to open the lid in order to add some trash from the kitchen when I sensed a hushed movement, an undetermined one, emanating from the gloomy interior. I could not make out what it was I had seen, but in the additional wild garden previously mentioned, the one I grow and cultivate between stomach and heart, a few primitive responses still linger, and although my eyes could not see and my mind could not understand, goose bumps ran up the length of my spine and the back of my head. My hands, as if of their own accord, quickly replaced the lid.

I closed it. I recomposed myself. I took a flashlight and opened the lid again. And indeed, curled up in the composter was a big black snake. A very big black snake. Judging by its thickness, I guessed it was more than seven feet long. The snake raised its head a little, tensed its body, and stared at me—and the blood froze in my veins. I left the composter open, withdrew, and watched it from a distance. The snake, as I had hoped, made its exit within minutes. What was it doing in the composter anyway? I suppose I threw something in there that attracted a rat or a mouse, and it, in turn, attracted the snake.

On the advice of my attorney I will add here a clarification and a warning: readers should not take my words as a recommendation to catch venomous snakes or fraternize with black widows.

43

Further Dangers

Aside from the scary creatures I have just described, who either live in the garden or pay it random visits, there is another species that stands out, one that is mostly amiable and useful but also potentially dangerous. I am talking about gardeners who suddenly appear for a visit. They neither bite nor sting, eat their way into tree trunks or gnaw at buds, and the truth is they are usually as congenial and pleasant as the flowers they grow. Advice can be garnered from them; bulbs, seeds, and tubers can be exchanged with them. But they often show up unannounced saying, "We heard you grow wildflowers, too."

"That's true," I say.

"So we've come to take a look."

And then they take a look. In other words, they wander through my garden, they survey and they scan. On the one hand, they do not trample over plants like other visitors, unable to distinguish nettles from anemones. On the other hand, it is easy to see how the expression on their faces becomes increasingly grim, particularly when they see a shrub that has been planted in a place where there is either insufficient sunlight or too much sunlight, or where the soil is unsuitable for growth.

After this, the examination begins. In a nonchalant kind of way, they quote names of plants I am unfamiliar with, like "saltmarsh aster" or "hawk's beard" and when I admit to not knowing these names they assume a critical expression. They are right. To my sorrow, I am not among those familiar with all two thousand and seven varieties of plants our country is blessed with—which is more than much larger countries have. I recognize every single plant in my garden, of course, but I am not as proficient in the flora of the Land of Israel as other enthusiasts, certainly not professional botanists, nor do I know as much as I would like to.

Most of the other gardeners are better than I at identifying plants, but the problem does not stop here. They also want to make sure I know this. When I tell them I have cat thyme, for example, they ask which cat thyme exactly, and since I do not know, and since the very term "cat thyme" amuses me, I invent names: I tell them I have curled-up cat thyme, or cross-legged cat thyme, curly cat thyme or cropped cat thyme. By the looks on the faces of my companions, I realize I have made a huge error, and by their reprimands I understand I should have said bowlegged cat thyme or bleached cat thyme or Cretan cat thyme. Indeed, such low humor is foreign and even abhorrent to them. I can tell by their grimaces that they are thinking I am unfit for the job and that a person like me is neither proficient nor serious enough to grow so much as a tuft of dog's-tooth grass.

In short, more than once I have surprised my interlocutors with my ignorance. Once, I recall, I was asked if I have queen mallow in my garden. Since I'd never heard that name, I said that the only mallow I know is the marshmallow growing in the bakery in Tivon where I buy caraway bread. The reaction was an expression of utter astonishment and patronizing scorn. Because anyone who does not know what queen mallow is, not to mention spotted-stalked tree mallow, little mallow, or Cretan hollyhock, is not worthy of joining the community of real wild gardeners. These, by the way, are mallow varieties I have never encountered in nature or in the recesses of my memory, but only in the index of a dictionary of plant names.

My inferiority regarding the identification of plants began at a traditional annual event called Tree Day held at the Nahalal Elementary School on the holiday of Tu BiShvat. The event had a sacred, routine structure: the pupils, the youngest of the young and the oldest of the old, from first grade to eighth grade, gathered in the nature room in small groups. Here a jar awaited them containing sprigs, flowers, stalks with leaves—according to season and species—of one hundred fifty different trees, shrubs, and flowers. A first grader was expected to identify ten of them, a second grader was expected to identify twenty, and an eighth grader—one hundred twenty!

This was a highly lucrative competition that afforded its winners eternal glory—albeit stardom that remained within the boundaries of Nahalal, but this little problem bothered no one: we all knew that nothing existed outside of the circle of Nahalal, certainly nothing of importance.

I was nine years old when we moved to Nahalal from Jerusalem. I was happy to move from city to country and I liked my new school, which to this day I remember as the nicest and best school I ever studied in. But the moniker "city boy" forever fluttered over my head, and to be a city boy and be called as much in the Nahalal of those days was to be inferior in every possible way. Add to this my lack of height, my narrow shoulders, my shortsightedness, and the fact that I was obsessed with reading—an unproductive custom—and you get a boy who was unable to integrate satisfactorily into the pioneering moshavnik experience.

It will therefore not come as a surprise that the first Tree Day filled me with horror. I knew that if I failed I would never live it down, and as is common in the collective agricultural movement, I would also bring eternal disgrace on my entire family.

The teacher of the fourth-grade class I studied in, Yaakov Matatia, prepared us for Tree Day in a very serious fashion. He personally knew every flower in the area and where it grew. On field days, he took us out to see them. We went to the so-called wadi—a small creek between Kfar Yehoshua and Nahalal—and to the "mountains," hills upon which the village of Timrat stands today. We went up and down the dense and humid Yagor stream, and we also went out on the streets of the moshav itself, because on Tree Day we were asked to identify not only wild plants but also ornamental plants that were popular in the collective agricultural movement: blue plumbago and Cape honeysuckle, Persian lilac, California pepper tree, Oriental arborvitae, also called ironed cypress in those days, bauhinia, privet, pittosporum, various cypresses and pines, and a further ornamental tree whose name made me really laugh: the brachychiton. My mother, who knew better than I all the names of the village plants—and, more important, its people—was also worried. Right away, she organized a crash course of her own on local flora: she went out with me to the fields, gathered sprigs and jars, and formulated plant ID tests and simulations that made my father chuckle to himself.

Tree Day arrived. I entered the nature room with a heavy, anxious heart and positioned myself in front of the plants we were to identify. In fourth grade we were supposed to know the names of at least forty trees and shrubs and flowers, and I began to slowly gather them together. I identified the sweet bay right away, recalling its leaves not only from the Carmel but from another habitat: my grandmother's jar of pickled herring. I identified the Canadian pine by its needles that grow in groups of three

rather than two. I also easily identified the aforementioned brachychiton—
who can forget a creature with such a funny name?

Somehow I also managed to conquer the hawthorn and two varieties
of rockrose, leaped over the hurdles of spiny broom and prickly burnet,
and even distinguished between the Mount Tabor oak and the Palestine
oak. I recognized the pungent false yellowhead because the nose remembers better than the eyes. But the African rue, which also has a distinctive,
strong fragrance, I missed.

Ultimately, I got through my first Tree Day by the skin of my teeth. I
identified forty-two plants and came last in my class. Our teacher consoled me, saying, "This is very good for your first time. Next year you'll
do better." But my mother said I ought to have identified a few more
plants.

Overconspicuous expertise in any subject is quite a credible indication
of the merit of those who are waving it around. But when it comes
to names of plants I also pay attention to the way those names are pronounced. For example, I am very cautious about people who say "irus"
instead of "iris," a common mistake in Hebrew. It does not bode well, and
if I may add: those, too, who say "vicia" by pronouncing the vowel with a
terminal stress instead of a consonant with a penultimate stress may well
harbor trouble under their hats.

Irises have a particularly problematic effect. I have a few Nazareth
irises in my garden, and every year they are kind enough to present me
with a flower or two, but I must admit that there is no real relationship
between us, and my garden does not boast the more elegant irises, such
as the Gilboa or coastal iris. They are too fancy for my taste, and their
blossoms look like the culmination of a particularly productive day in
the life of a milliner.

And not only that. I even dare to suggest that just as the iris is regarded as special and favored, so are some of those who love it: eccentric, somewhat strange people, even a species unto themselves, but I do not know whether it is the eccentricity that attracts them to the irises or the irises that make them so. Every garden influences its own influence on the soul, but iris growers and enthusiasts stand out from the crowd. It is not sufficient that they travel to the heart of darkness and beyond the seven mountains and seven seas in order to gaze at some endemic group of their precious irises; they also do things to them which I will define in clean language as unbecoming.

Let me try to explain: in comparison to my own minor self, who merely gathers seeds or wildflowers that grow in the garden, stores them, and plants them under enhanced conditions, these people carry out acts that are not worthy of printing here. In other words—and this "in other words" I will attempt to describe delicately—they participate in the actual fertilization. And if you still do not understand exactly what is going on there, I must reveal that they are in the habit of pollinating the object of their passion with bare hands, interfering in a crass and invasive manner with the flower's most intimate moments and body parts.

Come and see for yourself: a normal person courts the love of his life with flowers, whereas these people leave their loves at home and woo the flowers themselves, and they do this not only hidden away in the relative legitimacy of their private garden; they also invade the natural habitats of irises and harass them there. Some take the pollen receptacle of one iris and, with bated breath, use it to penetrate the stigma of another; others do it with a brush, and some are not satisfied unless they actually touch it with their hands: with the tips of their fingers they gather male pollen from one flower and then touch the female stigma of another flower. Whatever you call it, this is molestation of innocent, decent flowers, not to mention indecent assault.

I now return to the gardeners' visits. A further foreseeable danger from them is social interaction. In other words, after they see your garden they expect you to come and see theirs. A visit like this may be pleasant and constructive, but there are also dangers inherent within it, because the gardener may well find himself endlessly hosting and being hosted, and after that there will be weddings and circumcisions, and finally the worst of all—a sing-along, in which special emphasis is given to well-known Israeli folk songs about cyclamens, irises, and anemones. Let me remind you that all this happens because once, in a moment of weakness, you asked for and received a buttercup bulb or some crocus seeds.

A further foreseeable danger is the gardener who disdains you, your ineptitude and your amateurishness—which is not difficult to notice—and appoints himself your personal instructor. At first he gives good advice. Afterward he takes on a tone of instruction. Finally, he considers whether or not you followed his instructions and reprimands you if you did not.

Sometimes the teacher gives his student a prize in the form of a much desired bulb—an especially dark cyclamen or large anemone—but he also indicates where to place it in the earth, standing over the student as he plants it, saying, "Weed a little around it" or "Don't compress the soil further." After that, he returns to examine how the tuber he awarded his protégé is progressing and to claim that it is too deep or too shallow, that the acidity of the soil is unsuitable, and to tell anyone who asks that he is the one who exposed you to this magical world—most people who mispronounce "iris" also say "magical" when talking about wildflowers.

Aside from these other gardeners, most of my grievances against them stem from the fact that, although they usually know more and understand more than I do, occasionally someone arrives who has absolutely no idea about gardening, nor any interest in it, particularly when it comes to wild

gardens, but once they paid a visit to a garden like this during the flowering season and saw that it was good. They say "Wow!" and "Whoa!" and ask for seeds and bulbs and tubers. More than once I have given such people what they want, and the following year, when we happen to meet, I ask whether they were successful, and it turns out they neither planted nor sowed and have even forgotten where they put them—usually they leave them to boil to death in the trunk of the car—or they sow them and cover them up and a month later cement a path over them or lay a large stepping-stone on top of them. And right away I think of that bulb or that tuber, who were both so happy in my garden, and how I uprooted them and handed them over to that heartless son of a bitch who treated them the way he did, and my heart fills with anger and sorrow.

But none of that spoils the pleasure I derive from giving seeds and bulbs and tubers to those who really want them and who sow and plant them with care and consideration. At these times I offer advice and instruct where to plant. I stand over the person to ensure he is doing my bidding, I tell him the soil is too deep and not to compress it too much, and I come visit to see how germination is progressing, to remark remarks on the acidity of the soil, and to tell anyone who will listen that it was I who revealed to this same person the magical world of wildflowers.

44

Tree of the Field

Sometimes when I travel from my village to a city, a sad sight awaits me: a box of books resting on a fence or books thrown onto the sidewalk near a trash can, on occasion even inside the trash can. The significance is clear: another elderly cultured man or woman has passed away and no one is interested in the books he or she read and loved during their life. Not their sons or daughters, their grandsons or granddaughters, or the old bookstores or the public library.

Sometimes I rummage through these books and even take one or two, but coupled with my happiness at finding them are unavoidable thoughts of my own library. Many of its books will remain in the hands of my heirs, who are already casting yearning looks in their direction, and—if I may remark—are getting a little impatient. But then my thoughts wander to my second collection, the bulbs and tubers I have sowed and grown or brought here and set in the soil of my garden—what will become of them when the time comes? This is dependent, of course, on what happens to this little house. Who will live here? Lovers of gladioli and squills or fans of grassy lawns? And perhaps the house will be enlarged? Perhaps it will be razed to the ground, and a new and bigger house built on top of it?

Will anyone bother to save the bulbs and tubers by uprooting them before construction starts? Some of these bulbs and tubers I myself saved from construction sites and roadworks, before the tractors and steamrollers and cement mixers got there. Who will take them out of the ground and replant them? And where?

I do not consider myself a naturalist, nor do I hug trees or talk to bushes, but even mere amateurs like myself know that plants have mechanisms of sense and response and are more developed and sophisticated than developed and sophisticated mammals like ourselves are willing to attribute to other forms of life. There are many phenomena that prove this, and I will mention a few of them again: seeds that sprout or not according to external conditions, a flower that faces the sun and moves along with it, a creeper that seeks a good grip, a tree that inclines to one side in order to keep its distance from another tree. All these testify to their ability to sense and respond, to move toward and to feel attraction for what is desirable and a repulsion for what is not. But to escape a cement mixer or the bucket of a backhoe is not something plants can do. And the idea that my bulbs of cyclamen, anemone, gladiolus, and buttercup or tubers of sea squill or daffodil might be buried alive under a new house or stepping-stones causes me turmoil and literally makes me choke.

I visualize them sensing the thundering and quaking and pounding and pressure of heavy mechanical equipment, not to mention the penetration of blades and buckets and drills as they helplessly await their fate, because the most significant attribute of the plant is also its greatest limitation: although it is a living, breathing creature that drinks and eats and feels and responds, a plant cannot sprout legs, spread wings, fight, or flee.

Now here's a sad story: Near the Hemar wadi to the south of the Dead Sea once stood an acacia tree. It was large, beautiful, welcoming, and life-giving. Birds lived among its branches; all kinds of critters enjoyed its shade, from ants to hikers. More than once we stopped there, my friends and I, for a prehike breakfast, until one day we came and found it dead. Together with the egocentric disappointment we felt at that moment was also a sense of shock. There is something terrible in the sight of a dead tree still rooted in the ground, especially a dead tree you knew and loved while it was alive and visited at every opportunity.

The cause of death was earthwork that was taking place less than a mile away. The acacia tree lived on water brought to it by flooding that occurred two or three times a year, and a new crack in the earth was enough to divert the flow of those floods. In a case like this, animals trouble themselves to look for a new source of water, but plants are bound to the ground by their roots, and their fate is sealed.

Among humans, the word "rooted" is regarded in a positive light, but even the most rooted people can move from place to place. This is not so for plants. Their rootedness is their very essence. Everything derives from it, and it is this that rivets them to the ground and makes them so vulnerable, so very passive, easy to take advantage of and manipulate. Birds nest in them, reptiles and insects eat their leaves and their flesh, humans chop them up for their own needs, pick their fruit, tie swings to them, build children's playhouses in them, stick nails in them, and carve hearts on them. They suffer all this in silence. And in spite of their size and hardiness, they are helpless. They cannot flee or fight back.

In my wild garden there are a few indigenous terebinth trees remaining from the natural forest that flourished here before the village was built. The largest of these grows by the side of the road. Its trunk is split right at the base into two thick sections, its canopy is wide and dense and, I was told by an expert, this terebinth is two hundred years old. The tree and I share a special affinity because a few years ago I saved this tree from death, pure and simple, when I discovered a decision had been made to widen the village road a bit. The tree was to be felled.

When the authorities speak, I generally bow my head to them. Not because I am naturally obedient, but because I am aware of the life span of men and women in Israel, and there are pursuits I am not prepared to waste my energy on, nor the time remaining to me on this earth. This is not the case when someone tries to hurt those I love, particularly defenseless creatures such as the terebinth. As I mentioned earlier, trees cannot flee or fight back. A person with a saw and an ax in his hand can overcome the strongest and largest of trees.

The Bible relates to this matter in the following beautiful phrase: "Because man is a tree of the field." Many are familiar with these words, written by the poet Natan Zach and set to music by Shalom Hanoch, but it was not Natan Zach who coined this phrase. He took it from Deuteronomy, and today, thanks to his poetry, these words are an expression of feelings of identification and love for trees by man. Zach even stressed in his poem the points of resemblance between man and trees: both grow, both are eventually cut off from life, both are thirsty and burn. All this is well and good, not to mention intriguing, but the intentions of the author of Deuteronomy are not the same as those of the poet, and it is worthwhile examining them.

The full verse deals with a law forbidding the cutting down of trees around a city under siege, as is written: "When thou shalt besiege a city a long time, in making war against it to take it, thou shalt not destroy the trees thereof by wielding an axe against them; for thou mayest eat of them, but thou shalt not cut them down; for is the tree of the field man, that it should be besieged of thee?"

It is common knowledge that there are no punctuation marks in the Bible, and even the question mark at the end of the verse does not appear in the original Hebrew. When it is inserted here—as Rashi did so many years ago—it becomes apparent that the word "the," coming before "man," is not the definite article, as Natan Zach interpreted it, but the interrogative participle, and the verse does not describe the resemblance between man and trees but quite the opposite—something completely different. "Are the trees people, that you should besiege them?" In other words: Is the tree like a man, who can flee his enemies and find shelter behind walls? The answer is no, of course. Man is not a tree of the field, and a tree of the field is not a man, and the law forbidding the cutting down of trees around a city under siege is intended to save them.

Theoretically, this is the place to praise the Torah and admire its statutes, but unfortunately this is not so, and we cannot award ourselves the title "Righteous Among Trees." Reading on reveals that the prohibition on the felling of trees does not stem from concern for the fate of the tree but from the needs of man. The legislator of Deuteronomy adds: "Only the trees of which thou knowest that they are not trees for food, them thou mayest destroy and cut down, that thou mayest build bulwarks against the city that maketh war with thee, until it fall." In other words, the law forbidding the cutting down of trees applies only to fruit trees, because those trees may nourish the army during a time of war and be a legacy for the conquering nation, whereas non-fruit trees may be cut down to build instruments of siege.

Parenthetically, I would note that there is no difference between the Bible's essential conception of nature with man as the crowning glory and all the other creatures, plants, and animals meant to serve man and to be used by him. This appears in the words of God to Adam in the first chapter of Genesis, and also in Genesis Raba's Midrash, on the verse from chapter 2. Exactly like "man is a tree of the field" it opens beautifully with the following words: " 'No one to converse with [*siah*, which also means "bush"] in the field' (Gen. 2:5). All trees converse (*mesihim*), as it were,

with one another. Indeed, one may add, all trees converse with mortals."
But here, too, it continues badly: "all trees—created, as trees were, to provide pleasure for mortals."

A s for me and my terebinth, from the moment I realized its life was
in danger, remembering that biblical law will not stand by it since it
does not bear fruit, I took it upon myself to save the tree from death. First,
I hid a lock and shackle between its branches in order to chain myself to
the treetop when they came to chop it down. Second, I practiced climbing
the tree in order to get to the top in nimble fashion. And more important:
while the road wideners prepared to cut down the tree, I cut deals—I
approached everyone I possibly could at the Jewish National Fund and
local council and the Ministry of Agriculture, and it became clear that

sitting in all these places were people with God in their hearts, and no less important: they had the power which the terebinth and I lacked.

But why beat about the bush? The terebinth and I were shown mercy and its life was spared. To this day it stands at the end of my garden, green and full in summer, gray and bare when leaves fall in winter, with a myriad of cyclamens I planted blossoming around it. And sometimes, when the tree gets a little too big for its boots in the garden and its branches bow downward and stop me from walking straight-backed under it, I allow myself to give it a friendly prune, the same way the tree allows itself to scratch my balding pate.

45

Date and Carob

About fifty feet from the terebinth, I planted a carob tree. One day it will be as big as the terebinth, and these two giants will rub their branches together and compare crowns.

At the other end of the house I planted another carob, and I am happy to report that both are doing well, and I am waiting for them to grow tall and spread wide their branches. The natural shape of the carob is that of a massive bush whose trunk is concealed by the many dense branches which fork right out of the base of the trunk. But anyone who has ever hiked in Israel knows the carob that grows on pasture grounds. Its lower branches are pruned by the teeth of cows. The canopy of the tree begins where a cow with outstretched neck ends, so it is possible to sit in the carob's pleasant shade.

Another attribute of the carob is that it does not shed its leaves. In the summer it offers complete shade, and in winter it gives effective protection from rain. This tree induces a sense of home in me, a roof over my head, and since I do not have a herd of cows in my garden, I prune the carob myself into the shape of a large awning.

Oddly enough, the carob is not mentioned in the Bible. Some claim, however, that the word *herev,* "sword," in the final words of Isaiah 1:19–20, actually refers to *heruv,* meaning "carob": "If ye be willing and obedient, ye shall eat the good of the land: But if ye refuse and rebel, ye shall be devoured with the sword." Using this interpretation, the carob is regarded as meager and inferior food. And some say that the honey mentioned in the Bible does not only refer to the honey produced by bees but also to that produced by carob trees. Indeed, high-quality carob, the plump and juicy kind, oozes honey when split open, and these are the most delicious of fruits.

An even more interesting interpretation is that gerah, the biblical unit of weight, is actually a carob seed. The ancients noticed that each carob seed was of the exact same weight, and thus served as a reliable and convenient way of weighing gold and precious stones. In point of fact, there are linguists who claim that the term "karat" derived from this Hebrew word.

As for the tree itself—the carob is dioecious, meaning it produces both male and female plants. This matter need not disturb anyone, but the carob blossoms have a distinctive smell of human semen that spreads through the air. Some time ago, when I lived in Jerusalem, I found myself more than once walking or pedaling up Marcus Street in Talbieh. Large carob trees grew on either side of this street, and in the autumn months the males, whose blossoms are more abundant than those of the female, would give off an unmistakable odor. Not all passersby understand where all this living beauty comes from, and more than once I have witnessed an amusing spectacle: passersby pass by with different expressions on their upturned faces, each one according to his or her own life experiences and personal inclinations: Who would have believed it . . . Perhaps in the Katamon district of Jerusalem, but here in upper-class Talbieh?!

When I decided to plant carob in the garden, I planned ahead or, more precisely, because of the aforementioned odor, I resolved to plant female carobs rather than male ones. It is one thing to walk past a male carob at the prime of its life and to smile, and another thing altogether to plant one in your own garden and to live under the sublime and constant shadow of masculinity, autumn after autumn, year after year. Life presents enough humiliations. There is no need to bring more of them home.

The second thought I had was a regretful one, that I would not get to see those carobs at the pinnacle of their size and glory. But it was a fleeting thought and I overcame it easily. This is the way of the world, and just as there are those who preceded me in many other things, I was not the first to think this. The tale of our friend Honi the Circle Drawer, the bringer down of rain I mentioned previously, is well known. One day, he saw a man planting a carob tree. He asked how long it would take for the carob to bear fruit, and the man answered that it would take seventy years. He asked him if he would live that long and whether he would eat of the carob's fruit. The man answered: "Just as my forefathers planted trees for me, I am planting trees for my children." The rest of the story is common knowledge: Honi fell asleep for seventy years and when he awoke he saw the grandson of the planter eating the carob fruit. This nice story also has an instructive element to it, but it is established on an error: there is no need to wait seventy years for the carob to bear fruit. The tree will give copious quantities of fruit just a few years after being planted.

The third thought was where to plant it, a decision that needed good judgment and long-term planning. The carob is a large, wide tree; its foliage is dense and evergreen, creating full and constant shade underneath. It withholds light from its neighbors and prevents other plants from growing around it. It also roots deep into the earth and is difficult to transplant elsewhere unlike, for example, the olive tree.

After all these thoughts I planted my two carob trees each in its own place. They continue to develop nicely. I prune them in such a way that one can sit in their shade and, since they produce fruit, it is clear that the pollen of a male carob reaches them. It is albeit not as good a quality as I described above, but from time to time I taste it, and if a passerby stretches out a hand to pick one, I do not rebuke him. Let him eat, there is enough for everyone, and whatever falls to the ground will fertilize the soil. In this way the carob returns to the land that which it took.

While writing about female and male carobs, I recall a nice folktale about female and male dates that I read as a boy in *The Book of Legends* by Haim Nahmun Bialik and Yehoshua Hana Ravnitzky. The palm tree is also dioecious, having both male and female trees. Their growers are accustomed to extracting the pollen from the male palm and dusting it onto the flowers of the female in order to increase the degree of fertilization. The folktale I read is about a female date living in the Galilee area in a place known as Hamtam—perhaps the hot springs of Tiberias—who failed to produce fruit. A date expert by the name of Palmer saw her and said, " 'A male date she sees from Jericho and yearns for him in her heart.' They went and brought from him to graft her—and right away she produced fruit."

This sentence, "a male date she sees from Jericho and yearns for him in her heart" had a magical effect on me. First of all, I was happy to discover something that resembled Greek mythology in a Hebrew text. But the folktale itself, about a passionate female date and a beloved male date who are split apart by seventy miles, is evocative and beautiful because literature usually attributes such romantic passion to males, and also because the attributes of plants are highlighted here, chained by their roots to the ground.

There are three hearts in this story, and all three are beating wildly: the female date, who cannot unite with the distant male friend she yearns for in her heart, and perhaps the male date as well, as his heart senses her love from afar, and Palmer, who also has a warm and wise heart, who knows that plants feel not only hunger and thirst and heat and cold, light and dark, dryness and humidity, and the passing of hours and of seasons, but also love and passion, loneliness and yearning. All three are joined by the reader's heart, which fills with excitement as he or she reads.

And as for the grafting that is recounted there—it likely does not describe what we call the act of grafting as it is known today, but the hanging of a male inflorescence between those of a female, a practice that was well known in those days. The reader, who looks for a nice story in every connection of one word to another, derives a satisfaction that is more literary than botanic or agricultural, and that, too, is important.

46

"Oh Oh Virgin's Bower"

Many years ago, when I was a soldier, we were sent out on a long, hard navigation exercise in the Negev desert. We walked all night, and continued the next day, and in the afternoon we passed a throng of white broom, whose dense white blooms create the illusion that they are covered in snow. I moved aside, thrust my nose into one of them, opened my arms for a hug, and pressed myself against the branches. Then I shut my eyes, inhaled deeply, and a miracle occurred—the wonderful fragrance of white broom in blossom infused me with vitality and strength. It did not turn my feet into those of a deer, but it sustained and helped me. In the desert there are plants like this, whose lovely perfume or generous shade revives the wanderer as much as a rock pool full of good cold water.

To my sorrow, no white broom blossoms in my garden. To my delight, I am no longer in the military and only navigate in the desert when hiking. Even today, when I come across white broom there, I hasten to it, thrust my face into it, and inhale its fragrance with eyes closed. By the way, the same enjoyment can be derived on the dunes of the Plain of Sharon, where white broom blooms along the sides of the coastal road around the Alexander Stream, between Caesarea and Pardes Hanna, and also south of there, between Rishon LeZion and Ashdod. But the scent of white broom as it blooms in the desert is more intense, and the contradiction between this scent and the harsh environment is sharper.

A relative of the white broom flowers in my garden, a large bush by the name of rush broom that boasts fragrant yellow flowers. There are a few other wild plants that also exude an alluring fragrance: the Madonna lily, gladiolus, crocus, honeysuckle, styrax, spiny broom, sea daffodil, and sweet virgin's bower. In summer this last one blooms in a number of the wadis it is especially fond of in the Upper Galilee, and where it is particularly prevalent. The sweet virgin's bower is a vine. If it cannot find a tree to climb, the virgin bower creeps along the ground, climbs up itself, and creates a huge clump of blossoms. But if there is a tree, it climbs up, covering a great deal of the treetop, and, because these are summer days, the thousands of white flowers appear as snow at harvesttime.

The virgin's bower blossoms not only in nature but also in a nice story written by S. Yizhar, "Oh Oh Virgin's Bower." In reality, the virgin's bower only blossoms in season, but art is not obligated to laws of nature, and in Yizhar's story it blossoms whenever you read it, whatever the season. And there is but one important fact I cannot ignore, that Yizhar's bower is, in fact, simply virgin's bower, whereas the one that grows in my garden is sweet virgin's bower. I know this because Yizhar described a flower whose blossoms are yellowish and incline downward in order to protect against rain, whereas sweet virgin's bower has whitish blossoms that do not provide shelter against rain, since it flowers in the summer.

Yizhar first heard the cry "Oh Oh Virgin's Bower" from his nature studies teacher, Yehoshua Avizohar, who taught Yizhar and numerous others at the teacher's seminar in Bet Hakerem in Jerusalem. My father was also a student of his. He told me a nice story about Avizohar, who used to walk along the street, one foot on the sidewalk and the other on the road, wondering why he was limping. And indeed, Avizohar was known not only for his enthusiasm and his erudition but also for his absentmindedness. The story about his limp and similar episodes also appear in the story Yizhar wrote about Avizohar, but I will focus on the virgin's bower and the description he gave of the teacher's enthusiasm at the sight of the vine's blossoming in the wadi, where he was hiking with his students:

Our teacher, Avizohar, stopped, spread his arms out like Elijah the Prophet, and his blue eyes were as the brightness of the firmament as he shouted out from the depths of his heart, "Oh Oh," and we all stopped, and he continued to cry out there at the top of the hill, "Oh Oh Virgin's Bower," and we held our breath. "Oh Oh Virgin's Bower," our teacher Avizohar cried, his arms spread from one horizon to another toward the Temple of Jerusalem, "Oh Oh Virgin's Bower."

It is easy to distinguish a certain amount of ridicule in Yizhar's description of his teacher, a ridicule that stems both from Avizohar's mannerisms but also from the ridiculous name this flower goes by in the Hebrew language, *zalzelet,* which means "degradation," and which he utters here with such pathos. But there is also love and admiration for Avizohar's enthusiasm at the blossoms. He was, in fact, referring to virgin's bower and personally I prefer the sweet variety, because it flowers in summer, when flowers are few and far between, and its blossoming has a wonderful fragrance.

I always wanted a virgin's bower like this in the garden but did not know how to find one. And then one day, while hiking near Hurfeish, I saw a Druze farmer tilling his olive grove. There were a few vines of virgin's bower that had climbed and blossomed on the stone wall of the grove, and I stopped to look at them and smell their blossoms. Lying close by on the ground was a small virgin's bower that had been uprooted by the blades of the plow.

I asked the farmer if I could take it. "Do as you please, but it'll die," the farmer replied. He showed me that the root had been severed before it had time to branch out and spread through the soil. I decided to cut short the hike. I wrapped the torn root in a rag soaked in water, turned the ambulance siren on, and drove home. Once there, I hospitalized the virgin's bower in a large plant pot and then watered it copiously.

After several days the branches wilted and dried up, but I did not give up. I pruned it and continued watering. A few more days passed and the stalk—I do not know if this is the correct term here, but it certainly cannot be called a trunk—completely withered. I cut it to a height of about eight inches above the soil and continued watering the cutting.

For three whole months I watered this dead thing twice a week. I had already begun to poke fun at myself and even to question my own mental health, when one day a green bud burst forth from this dried-up virgin's bower! I could hardly believe my eyes, but a few days later another bud appeared. The buds became leaves, and then new vines appeared and sprouted more leaves, and the virgin's bower, like the rod of Aaron HaCohen—which "brought forth buds and bloomed blossoms"—was resurrected!

I transplanted the plant to a bigger pot, and the next summer Madame Virgin's Bower was already climbing up the trellis I had fixed for her—and blossoming! If there were punctuation marks for pride and happiness, I would have used them here. But because there are none, I have used what I can, an exclamation mark.

There is a nice ending to Yizhar's story of Avizohar and the virgin's bower, in which he describes the positive influence upon those who utter the cry of "Oh Oh Virgin's bower," even if this person is not a teacher of nature studies nor standing in front of such a plant.

He even urged the reader to try it. "Try for a moment and you will be convinced," he writes in the story. "Arise, stand up wherever you are, arise and stand up and stretch out your arms to your sides, and try calling out in a loud voice and with all your heart like this: Oh Oh Virgin's bower— and see what happens."

I chuckled when first reading this. But a few days later, when my spirits were in need of uplifting and I was alone in the house, I got to my feet and stood by the large window that faces the Carmel. I stood up, stretched my arms out to my sides, and called out: "Oh Oh Virgin's bower!"—and it happened. Yizhar's recommendation-observation came true. Since then, every time I feel the need, I get up and stand with my arms outstretched and call out in a loud voice and with all my heart: "Oh! Oh! Virgin's bower!" I do so most of the year by the window, and in the flowering season—facing the virgin's bower itself. Either way—it happens. It really does.

Try it for yourself. When your heart is overflowing or, on the contrary, your heart is struggling and cringing—you, too, should call out in a loud voice and with all your heart like this: "Oh! Oh! Virgin's bower!"—and just see what happens.

47

The Lemon Tree

At the beginning of this book I spoke about my lemon tree—how I found it dying near the house when I first came here, how I brought it back to life, and how it recompensed me with its fragrant blossoming, delicious fruit, and unparalleled limoncello. But a dozen years passed, and after enjoying old age, the tree began to decline. Many leaves fell from the tree, most of its branches withered, and its blossoms were meager and melancholic and put forth precious little fruit.

My friend Puyu, the elderly tree planter, had passed away and was no longer here to give me advice. Therefore, I repeated what he had told me to do to that same lemon tree the first time we met, but this time I suffered defeat: I pruned again—in vain. I fertilized and watered it—and the lemon tree waned. Finally, I consulted with other experts who even graced the tree and me with a visit—they came, sawed off a branch, examined the dry core, and held counsel in hushed tones beside the patient. They whispered together, asked me questions, just like doctors in a hospital who address the relative rather than the aged patient himself: "How old is he?" But it was not I who planted the tree, and I was unable to give them an accurate answer.

In the end, they advised me to cut down the tree and plant a new one in its place. But I did not dare do that. I said to myself: Winter will come, rain will fall, spring will bloom, and perhaps God will remember my poor old lemon tree; He will come visit and perform a miracle.

No miracle occurred, but a few days later an unfamiliar couple knocked at my door and asked to come in. The woman was very excited. This is the house, she told me, where she spent her childhood and adolescence, and she wanted to show it to her beloved. I invited them to come in, and after she had shown him what she wanted to show and told him what she wanted to tell, I asked her about the lemon tree—did she know who planted it and in which year? She said her father planted it a few years before she was born and, according to her childhood memories, the tree was full grown.

I plucked up the courage to ask her another question, an impolite but necessary one, and figured out that my lemon tree was more than sixty years old—a grand old age for a citrus tree—and those experts were right, the tree must be felled and a new one planted in its place.

I did it with heavy heart and light hands. The tree was so feeble and falling apart that some of the felling was achieved by simply jolting and pulling it. After the deed was done, I went to a plant nursery to buy a new lemon tree. While alive, my lemon tree gave me one yield of fruit per year. Now I resolved to take a variety that bears fruit twice a year, and I chose a large sapling, because I, too, am a rather old lemon tree, and I do not want to wait too long for it to bear fruit.

I invited my eldest granddaughter, who was five and a half years old at the time, to the planting ceremony. A child should participate in a tree-planting ceremony so that she can grow with the tree, and beside the tree, and will know to plant trees herself. We did not plant the new lemon tree where the old one had stood, in case there was something wrong with the soil. We chose a new place based on its distance from neighboring trees, hours of sun and shade, depth of soil, and distance from the kitchen. We discussed all this, and finally my granddaughter determined the spot: "Here!" And I stuck my pitchfork in the ground.

Happily, this time I did not damage the underground irrigation pipe. I dug the planting hole, we filled it with water, and when the ground had absorbed it all we filled it again, and after that we covered the ground with compost from my composter and added another thin layer of soil. I explained to both children, my granddaughter and the sapling, that today we ought to call the compost *d'shonet* and the composter *madshen,* and I discovered that a child of five and a half and a two-year-old lemon tree also have trouble pronouncing these new words.

We added more water, positioned the sapling in the well, and then took a step back to ensure it was standing straight and fitted in with its surroundings. We considered it from a variety of angles, and when the three of us were completely satisfied, I cut and removed the bag in which the sapling's roots were packed, and we heard it sigh heavily with relief.

We raked and covered the clump of roots in the earth, firmed the soil a little—the paces and steps of a five-and-a-half-year-old girl are the finest firming method possible for the sapling, exactly like the perfect pressure applied to the aching back of her grandfather in those days. We watered the sapling once again, stuck three supporting poles around it, and lashed the sapling to them with strips of material, because rope can injure the sapling's outer bark. We did not tighten them, since the sapling needs to move a little in the wind, otherwise it will not develop muscles nor thicken or gain strength as it should.

The planting is over. I have a new lemon tree in the garden. I still feel sad at the sight of the empty space where that old-timer stood, but I am planning to fill it with a grape arbor. The young lemon tree has acclimatized well and is used to its neighbors and the garden. Soon it will grow bigger and bear fruit. And one day my granddaughter will tell her own granddaughter that the time has come to plant a new lemon tree in its place, because this one is already sixty years old.

About the Author

One of Israel's most celebrated novelists, Meir Shalev was born in 1948 on Nahalal, Israel's first moshav. His books have been translated into more than twenty-five languages and have been best sellers in Israel, Holland, and Germany. He is also a columnist for the Israeli daily *Yedioth Ahronoth*. His honors include the National Jewish Book Award and the Brenner Prize, one of Israel's top literary awards, for *A Pigeon and a Boy*. He has been named a Chevalier de l'Ordre des Arts et des Lettres by the French government. Shalev lives in Jerusalem and in the north of Israel.

About the Translator

Joanna Chen is the translator of *Less Like a Dove* (Shearsman Books, 2017) and *Frayed Light* (Wesleyan University Press, 2019). She writes a column for the *Los Angeles Review of Books*. Her work can be read at www.joannachen.com.

About the Illustrator

Refaella Shir is an Israeli artist who resides in Montreal. She studied art in Israel, Canada, and the United States and has exhibited internationally. In 2009 she illustrated an anthology of poems published in Israel. Her work can be viewed at www.refaellashir.com.

Note on the Type

This book was set in Minion, a typeface produced by the Adobe Corporation specifically for the Macintosh personal computer and released in 1990. Designed by Robert Slimbach, Minion combines the classic characteristics of old-style faces with the full complement of weights required for modern typesetting.

Typeset by North Market Street Graphics,
Lancaster, Pennsylvania

Printed and bound by C&C Offset,
China

Designed by Betty Lew

Cyclamen

Snowdrop

Gladiolus

Sorrel

Spiny Broom

Syrian
Cornflower–Thistle

Hawk's Beard

Corn Poppy

Bristly Hollyhock

Agrostemma

Bougainvillea

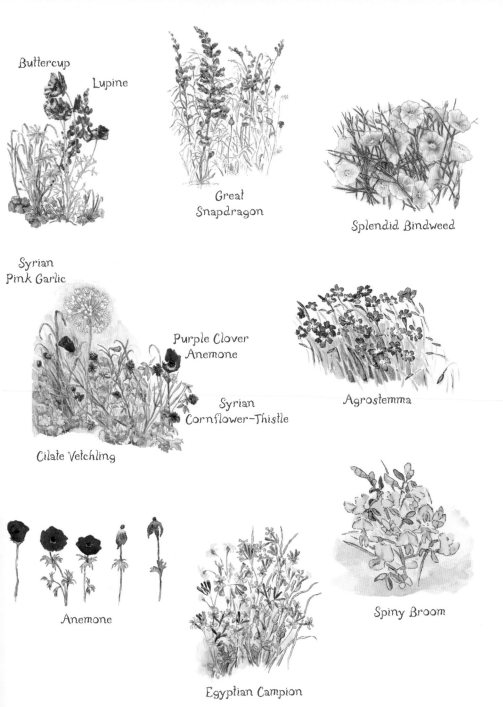

Buttercup

Lupine

Great
Snapdragon

Splendid Bindweed

Syrian
Pink Garlic

Purple Clover
Anemone

Syrian
Cornflower-Thistle

Agrostemma

Cilate Vetchling

Anemone

Egyptian Campion

Spiny Broom